D1612751

Julian Barnes

Manchester University Press

Contemporary British Novelists

Series editor Daniel Lea

already published

J. G. Ballard   Andrzej Gasiorek
Pat Barker   John Brannigan
A. S. Byatt   Alexa Alfer and Amy J. Edwards de Campos
Jim Crace   Philip Tew
James Kelman   Simon Kövesi
Iain Sinclair   Brian Baker
Graham Swift   Daniel Lea
Irvine Welsh   Aaron Kelly
Jeanette Winterson   Susana Onega

Julian Barnes

Peter Childs

Manchester University Press
Manchester and New York
distributed in the United States exclusively by Palgrave Macmillan

Copyright © Peter Childs 2011

The right of Peter Childs to be identified as the author of this work has been asserted by him in accordance with the Copyright, Designs and Patents Act 1988.

Published by Manchester University Press
Oxford Road, Manchester M13 9NR, UK
and Room 400, 175 Fifth Avenue, New York, NY 10010, USA
www.manchesteruniversitypress.co.uk

Distributed in the United States exclusively by
Palgrave Macmillan, 175 Fifth Avenue, New York,
NY 10010, USA

Distributed in Canada exclusively by
UBC Press, University of British Columbia, 2029 West Mall,
Vancouver, BC, Canada V6T 1Z2

British Library Cataloguing-in-Publication Data
A catalogue record for this book is available from the British Library

Library of Congress Cataloging-in-Publication Data applied for

ISBN   978 0 7190 8106 4 hardback

First published 2011

The publisher has no responsibility for the persistence or accuracy of URLs for any external or third-party internet websites referred to in this book, and does not guarantee that any content on such websites is, or will remain, accurate or appropriate.

Typeset 10/12pt FFScala by Graphicraft Limited, Hong Kong
Printed in Great Britain by the MPG Books Group, UK

Contents

Series editor's foreword   *page* vi

Acknowledgements   vii

List of abbreviations   viii

Introduction: Pleasure in form   1

1   About to be less deceived: *Metroland*   19

2   Silly to worry about: *Before She Met Me*   34

3   What happened to the truth is not recorded:
    Flaubert's Parrot   46

4   Intricate rented world: *Staring at the Sun*   60

5   Safe for love: *A History of the World in 10½ Chapters*   71

6   Tell me yours: *Talking It Over* and *Love, etc*   84

7   We won't get fooled again: *The Porcupine*   98

8   History doesn't relate: *England, England*   108

9   Retrospectively imagined memorials: *Cross Channel* and
    The Lemon Table   126

10 Conviction and prejudice: *Arthur & George*   139

Select bibliography   159

Index   163

Series editor's foreword

Contemporary British Novelists offers readers critical introductions to some of the most exciting and challenging writing of recent years. Through detailed analysis of their work, volumes in the series present lucid interpretations of authors who have sought to capture the sensibilities of the late twentieth and twenty-first centuries. Informed, but not dominated, by critical theory, *Contemporary British Novelists* explores the influence of diverse traditions, histories and cultures on prose fiction, and situates key figures within their relevant social, political, artistic and historical contexts.

The title of the series is deliberately provocative, recognising each of the three defining elements as contentious identifications of a cultural framework that must be continuously remade and renamed. The contemporary British novel defies easy categorisation and, rather than offering bland guarantees as to the current trajectories of literary production, volumes in this series contest the very terms that are employed to unify them. How does one conceptualise, isolate and define the mutability of the contemporary? What legitimacy can be claimed for a singular Britishness given the multivocality implicit in the redefinition of national identities? Can the novel form adequately represent reading communities increasingly dependent upon digitalised communication? These polemical considerations are the theoretical backbone of the series, and attest to the difficulties of formulating a coherent analytical approach to the discontinuities and incoherencies of the present.

Contemporary British Novelists does not seek to appropriate its subjects for prescriptive formal or generic categories; rather it aims to explore the ways in which aesthetics are reproduced, refined and repositioned through recent prose writing. If the overarching architecture of the contemporary always eludes description, then the grandest ambition of this series must be to plot at least some of its dimensions.

Daniel Lea

Acknowledgements

The writing of this book was supported by the generous grant of an Oneal fellowship by the Harry Ransom Research Centre at The University of Texas in Austin, which enabled me to conduct research for a month into its extensive Barnes archive of manuscript drafts, correspondence, and other papers. The HRC holdings to which I had access in 2008 are divided into two archives dating from 2002 and 2006. The 2002 deposits comprise 19 boxes, three oversize boxes and one oversize folder divided into four series: Works; Articles; Correspondence 1971–98; Career related material. The 2006 deposits are arranged into 12 boxes, one oversize box and one oversize folder split into two series: Works 1996–2006 and Correspondence plus other papers 1960 to 2006. Observations gleaned from this research pepper this analysis of Barnes's novels and inform my appraisal of his aims and techniques. I would like to thank Daniel Lea and Matthew Frost for commissioning this book and the influential Barnes critics who have gone before me, pointing directions for the discussions in this study, particularly Merritt Moseley, Vanessa Guignery, Matthew Pateman, Frederick M. Holmes, and Sebastian Groes. Finally, I would like to thank Claire Smith for her research work into the bibliographic record.

Peter Childs

List of abbreviations

The following abbreviations are used for references to these editions of the works of Julian Barnes. (Date of first publication given where a later edition is used.)

M *Metroland* (1980; London: Robin Clark, 1981)
BS *Before She Met Me* (1982; London: Picador, 1986)
FP *Flaubert's Parrot* (1984; London: Picador, 1985)
SS *Staring at the Sun* (1986; New York: Harper & Row, 1988)
HW *A History of the World in 10½ Chapters* (London: Jonathan Cape, 1989)
CC *Cross Channel* (1995; London: Picador, 1996)
TO *Talking It Over* (1991; London: Picador, 1992)
P *The Porcupine* (1992; London: Picador, 1993)
LL *Letters from London: 1990–5* (London: Picador, 1995)
EE *England, England* (London: Jonathan Cape, 1998)
LE *Love, etc* (London: Jonathan Cape, 2000)
SD *Something to Declare* (London: Picador, 2002)
LT *The Lemon Table* (2004; London: Picador, 2005)
AG *Arthur & George* (London: Jonathan Cape, 2005)
NF *Nothing to Be Frightened of* (London: Jonathan Cape, 2008)

Introduction: Pleasure in form

The contemporary is peculiarly difficult to write about because negligible hindsight and questions of proper context make assessments and judgements more than usually vulnerable. Appraising the work of a living writer is unlikely to cover the entire oeuvre because fresh works may appear. In the case of Julian Barnes, it is also true that he prefers not to be written about by critics, partly because it makes him feel entombed rather than a living voice. As pertinently, Barnes would prefer not to be mediated by the entire book industry. He has said:

> In an ideal world, a novelist – me, for instance – would write a book, readers would become aware of it by word of mouth, and, after reading it, they would send a small donation to the writer at a secret address, these donations adding up to enough to keep the writer alive. No publishers, no reviewing, no profiles, just the purest contact between reader and book, and the fullest ignorance about the writer . . . Only the words should count.[1]

This belief in the importance of 'the words' alone is a viewpoint that Barnes shares with the nineteenth-century French novelist Gustave Flaubert. It is well known that Flaubert is not only a principal subject of Barnes's most famous book but also the writer most admired by him. Both authors indeed share a taste for irony and Flaubert sought an objectivity in art that Barnes clearly appreciates highly because it signals a purity of aesthetic approach. However, Barnes himself seems to be a highly subjective artist at times, and one who aims for something different from the quasi-scientific objectivity of a higher realism or a naturalism that has been pursued by other Flaubertian acolytes such as Émile Zola. Judging from the commentary in Barnes's work, if not always the content, what he appears to aim for in his fiction is less objectivity than an effect closer to truth. Similarly, he does not aim for an absence of personality in the writer, but he would favour anonymity, leaving just 'the words' for the reader. Despite this, Barnes published in 2008 a book presented as a memoir: *Nothing to Be Frightened of.* The book oscillates between anecdotal illustration and a review of the comments artists and thinkers have made on the subject of death, epitomising the conversational, essayistic style at which Barnes excels. Little of his life is revealed but the book is scattered with personal reflections on private conversations and family dynamics.

Flaubert 'forbade posterity to take any personal interest in him' (FP, p. 16) and clearly Barnes would for the most part wish the same, even while he is alive. However, some biographical detail will provide a context to the novels without encouraging the reader to 'chase the writer' (FP, p. 12). Barnes was born on 19 January 1946 in Leicester, to Albert Leonard and Kaye Scoltock Barnes, both now dead. His only sibling is an older brother, Jonathan, a philosopher specialising in the ancient Greeks, for whose book *Coffee with Aristotle* Julian Barnes has written a foreword. Their parents were from north Midlands families and both worked as school teachers of French. The family moved to Acton in West London when Julian Barnes was an infant and then to Northwood when he was ten. He made his first trip to France with his family in 1959 and has come to be considered a Francophile, like his brother, who has taught at the Sorbonne as well as at Geneva and Oxford universities.

Educated at the private City of London School for boys, Julian Barnes became a suburban commuter, like Chris in *Metroland*. Reminding the reader of the pilot Prosser in *Staring at the Sun*, the family rented out the top floor of their house to military air personnel, Barnes's father having been an adjutant in the air force in India. As a boy, Barnes's reading included Rimbaud, Baudelaire, Voltaire, and Verlaine, and he has said that 'the area of French literature I respond most to is the sceptical, pragmatic, realist, untheoretical strand represented by writers such as Montaigne, Voltaire and Flaubert'.[2] An eclectic reader, he has listed his favourite books as: 'Shakespeare to the *Oxford English Dictionary* to the *Michelin Guide to France* to *Flaubert's Letters* to Jane Grigson's *Vegetable Book*'.[3]

Barnes won a scholarship to study Modern Languages at Magdalen College, Oxford, graduating in 1968. After university he sat exams for the civil service but decided not to accept the job he was subsequently offered as a tax inspector. Instead, he took to unemployment before getting a job as a lexicographer for the *Oxford English Dictionary* supplement. He worked on the *OED* for three years and while he was there wrote an unpublished literary guide to Oxford, though his university experience fell short of his expectations. He then trained to become a lawyer, while writing occasional book reviews.

Despite passing his Bar finals in 1974 Barnes went on to become a freelance journalist, working as a reviewer and assistant literary editor for the *New Statesman* and contributing editor for the *New Review*, where he wrote the Greek Street column under the name Edward Pygge. In 1979 he married the literary agent Pat Kavanagh, with whom he remained until her death in 2008. At the *New Statesman* he worked under Martin Amis, a close friend until they fell out in the mid-1990s when Amis dropped Kavanagh as his agent.

In 1979 Barnes also began a seven-year stint as a TV critic, first for the *New Statesman*. After employment as the deputy literary editor at *The Sunday Times* (1980–82), and writing as the *Tatler*'s restaurant critic under the peudonym Basil Seal (a recurring figure in Evelyn Waugh's novels), he succeeded Clive James as *The Observer* TV critic, and continued in that post up to 1986. By this time he had become a highly praised novelist and could start to think about turning to writing fiction full time with the huge literary success of *Flaubert's Parrot* in 1984.

Barnes's first novel, *Metroland*, was published in 1980 to very positive critical reviews. It went on to win the Somerset Maugham Award for a debut novel. To 2010, nine other novels have followed as well as two books of essays, a memoir, and two collections of short stories, plus a book on cookery, numerous introductions to works by other writers, and a translation of the notebook of his illness *In the Land of Pain* by the French novelist Alphonse Daudet (1840–97).

Under the pseudonym Dan Kavanagh, Barnes has additionally written four crime novels, all of which appeared in the 1980s at a time when Barnes seemed still a little unsure of his future direction: literary novelist, crime writer, journalist, editor or some combination of the above. The first *Duffy* private detective story appeared in 1980 and focuses on the Soho area of London and its sex trade, investigated by Barnes's eponymous hero, a bisexual ex-policeman turned private detective. The second book, *Fiddle City* (1981), is set at London's Heathrow airport and features Duffy's investigation of a smuggling operation. *Putting the Boot in* (1985) turns to English minor-league football, and *Going to the Dogs* (1987) to questions of class and greyhound racing. While they focus on quintessentially English milieux the novels are less like traditional British detective stories than hard-boiled American crime fiction, with Nick Duffy as a jaded gumshoe for hire in the manner of writers such as Dashiell Hammett and Raymond Chandler. Though they are enjoyable pot-boilers, for a point of British comparison the *Duffy* novels lack the depth and resonance of Dennis Potter's contemporaneous TV scripts for *The Singing Detective* (1986), which has at its centre a writer called Philip Marlowe and is similarly indebted to Chandler and Hammett. The *Duffy* books are well-plotted, quickly written vernacular novels in a popular genre that could have occupied Barnes if he had not had success as a different kind of author. They do show more clearly the moral streak that runs through Barnes's other works and exhibit an ease with popular culture as well as Barnes's considerable skill at adapting his voice to different genres and settings.

By contrast the writing of *Metroland* drew from Barnes's childhood and youth, including his experiences while living in Murray Road, Northwood, close to the mainline station and the Metropolitan Tube line. *Metroland* took about eight years to write and is one of the most conventional of Barnes's novels. Influences are already clear here, not only from French literature but from the English vein of provincial and suburban poets, such as Betjeman and Larkin, to the great European writers of the nineteenth and early twentieth centuries, and recent American social anatomists like John Cheever and John Updike.

In a profile for the *Big Issue* publication, Barnes answered the question 'What do you most dread?' with this statement: 'The usual things: death, pain, loneliness.' These deepest anxieties seem to encapsulate one set of concerns that run through Barnes's work. *Staring at the Sun*, his fourth novel, is a narrative in many ways about looking death in the face, and *Nothing to Be Frightened of* is primarily about living with mortality. But there are other aspects to his work, and these feed off and on the things that for Barnes make life worth living: art, love and an open curiosity about the world that informs and accompanies his diverse publications, from the *Duffy* detective stories to essays on philosophy, food, or Flaubert. His literary tastes are broad and in 2008, for example, he commented that he was currently working on 'an edition of the Irish short-story writer Frank O'Connor, a long piece about Penelope Fitzgerald, an introduction to Clough's "Amours de Voyage" '.[4]

The comment that perhaps best prepares the reader for the breadth of Barnes's writing was one he made in 1992 to Mira Stout: 'In order to write, you have to convince yourself that it's a new departure not only for you but for the entire history of the novel.'[5] This in some ways accounts for the balance between familiarity and newness struck by each Barnes novel. Richard Bradford thus decides that Barnes might be 'the best-known practitioner of this curious compromise between the customary and the aberrant'.[6] His novels can sometimes seem like conversational forays that develop a line of thought about society and culture into all kinds of fictional avenues but they are also often formally unusual and almost perversely experimental.

Barnes's fiction reflects a wide array of approaches but settles on a combination of social satire, Swiftian irony, and experimentation. He is also influenced by the strain of melancholy that runs through such English poets as Hardy, Housman, and Larkin, elegising as much as eulogising over existence's inability to deliver wish-willed expectations, with life marked by a sense of loss and disappointment but also of continued hope underlined by stoicism and pragmatism. Love and life fail but there is much that is beautiful and amusing in the mismatch between human beings' reach and grasp. Frederick Holmes notes that 'Although his books are informed by pessimism, the experience of reading them is far from dispiriting. They are richly textured, aesthetically accomplished, highly entertaining productions, fuelled by clear-sighted intelligence, crackling wit, emotional depth, and a broad imaginative sympathy.'[7]

For the most part, Barnes is a comic novelist. However, this does not mean that his books particularly aim to make the reader laugh or that they are not serious in intent. As Matthew Pateman observes, there is a balance to the tragicomic irony: 'Often regarded as witty and clever, Barnes's novels are also subdued melancholic meditations.'[8] His stylistic range is greater than such British predecessors as Evelyn Waugh, Kingsley Amis, and Angus Wilson and he engages with the form of the novel more than these earlier writers. His pre-eminent influences are both Anglophone and European and include philosophers, poets, and essayists as well as novelists. He writes out of a tradition that indeed sees little need to distinguish between kinds of writing, which differentiation is largely a convenience for the reader, not a straitjacket for the writer. Barnes has penned introductions, essays, TV reviews, criticism, and texts like *The Pedant in the Kitchen*, about his experience cooking from recipes. The picture this book of culinary anecdotes and observations paints of Barnes, as someone requiring precise instructions and timings, is echoed in *Talking It Over* when Gillian finds Stuart has a detailed timetable for cooking her a meal at his flat (TO, pp. 74–5). However, the meal is a simple shoulder of lamb with frozen peas, so Barnes's own interest in fine dining is better represented in that novel, unsurprisingly, by Oliver's contrasting *tagine* of lamb with apricots (TO, p. 115).

Ironic comedy and false memory are two of the poles around which Julian Barnes's work revolves, and this book will have occasion to touch repeatedly on each. 'Memento ergo sum' is the reformulation of the Cartesian *cogito* advanced by Brian Moore's Mary Dunne, and this is a useful starting point for considering Barnes on memory.[9] If the past is alive for us in the present because we remember it, Barnes's fiction would suggest that it is not necessarily the past that we remember. The versions and details that inhabit memories are mutable and changeable. Recollections fashion a current sense of identity and arguably vice versa, but for Barnes the most important aspect to memory is that it is imaginative. 'They say that as you get older, you remember your earliest years better', remarks Oliver in *Talking It Over* (TO, p. 15) and Barnes turns to memory more and more in his later fiction. *England, England, Cross Channel*, and *Arthur & George*, to name three works, are deeply concerned with the workings and mechanisms of retrospection, recollection, and remembrance, which Barnes discusses explicitly in his memoir, *Nothing to Be Frightened of*. Here loss of memory is linked to loss of identity and personal annihilation, but Barnes is as interested in the creative as in the defective aspects to remembering, which link to the imaginative aspects of making fiction.

Barnes's understanding of memory connects clearly with his most characteristic approach to fiction and its relation to alternative modes of writing: generic fabulation. With regard to *England, England*, Barnes describes fabulation this way: 'convincing ourselves of a coherence between things that are largely true and things that are wholly imagined.'[10] He also refers to history as a 'soothing fabulation' in *A History of the World in 10½ Chapters* (HW, p. 242), underlining the processes of construction and reconstruction in shaping the past, whether individual or collective. Elsewhere in interview he expands on this viewpoint: 'History, that controlling narrative of the literate, was spun from the lies of the victors (plus the false excuses of the defeated); the selective memory of survivors; the skewed emphasis of the powerful.'[11] In a different conversation he explains further that fabulation

> is a medical term for what you do when a lot of your brain has been destroyed either by a stroke or by alcoholism, or that sort of thing. And – it's rather gratifying for a novelist – the human mind can't exist without the illusion of a full story. So it fabulates and convinces itself that the fabulation is as true and concrete as what it 'really' knows. Then it coherently links the real and the totally imagined in a plausible narrative.[12]

In literary criticism, the term fabulation was brought to prominence by Robert Scholes in his 1967 study *The Fabulators*, where it was used to refer to fiction by such writers as Kurt Vonnegut, Iris Murdoch, Lawrence Durrell, and John Barth. Though there are other notable differences, Barnes's fiction can be aligned with some of the approaches used by this group of novelists in a variety of ways, particularly in terms of experimentation with genre, form, and style, blurring distinctions between categories of writing rather than between, for example, reality and fantasy (though that is an interest of a story such as 'The survivor'). There is a connection here with postmodernism, which overtook Scholes's term in popular discussions of postwar fiction and would be used to describe work by several of the same writers.

In his collection of essays *The Novelist at the Crossroads* (1971) David Lodge cites fabulation as fiction's opposite literary direction to realism. Fabulation takes cues from other narrative forms than those that aim at verisimilitude. While Barnes does not often veer into many kinds of experimentation with modes of representation, he is one of the foremost contemporary British writers to explore the variety of forms of writing that the novel can encompass. In expanding on Scholes's use of the fundamental division between two antithetical modes of narrative, the empirical which tends towards the real, and the fictional, which tends towards the ideal, combined with an argument that the two become synthesised to form the novel in the eighteenth century, Lodge contends that this broadbrush theory may be in some ways reductive but at least 'accounts for the great variety and inclusiveness of the novel form'. The modern novel thus is pushed at different times towards allegory, history/autobiography, or romance, with realism as the synthesising mode for the others.[13] Scholes argues that his writers exemplify a trend to veer away from realism towards the ideal mode, exploring the novels' aspects of romance and allegory rather than history and mimesis.

In his own theory on contemporary fiction at the start of the 1970s, Lodge effectively places the novelist at a crossroads of experimentation and realism, and while the latter inspires 'anyone whose imagination has been nurtured by the great realistic novelists of the past', the path of realism appears to hold little for those who are interested in literature's potential: 'Scholes's fabulators, for instance, play tricks on their readers, expose their fictive machinery, dally with aesthetic paradoxes, in order to shed the restricting conventions of realism, to give themselves freedom to invent and manipulate.'[14] Combining these observations brings Julian Barnes's fictions closer into focus as texts that are indebted to the foremost achievements of classic realism ('*Middlemarch* is probably the greatest English novel')[15] but are mostly inspired by the display of technique in, for examples, Flaubert's scrupulous linguistic precision or Ford Madox Ford's artful use of narratorial artlessness in *The Good Soldier*. Barnes's interest in fabulation appears to lie in its mixture of approaches to fiction derived from reality and imagination, which is a characteristic of mental functioning encoded by the novelist in fictional experimentation to illustrate the complexity of a flawed but highly creative human relationship with experience. In such a reading, Barnes's second novel *Before She Met Me*, for example, is a book about slippage between reality and textual analysis in the construction of personal narrative: an imperfect jigsaw puzzle of attempted objective and willed subjective observation, insight and extrapolation, invention and fact.

In his 1979 book *Fabulation and Metafiction*,[16] Scholes offers the following comments on his term, deciding that 'fabulation' expresses 'the sense that the positivistic basis for traditional realism had been eroded, and that reality, if it could be caught at all, would require a whole new set of fictional skills'.[17] He expands by saying that

> Fabulation, then, means not a turning away from reality, but an attempt to find more subtle correspondences between the reality which is fiction and the fiction which is reality. Modern fabulation accepts, even emphasizes, its fallibilism, its inability to reach all the way to the real, but it continues to look toward reality. It aims at telling such truths as fiction may legitimately tell in ways which are appropriately fictional.[18]

This describes the difference between the seriousness in *Metroland* of Christopher's fascination with Baudelarian correspondences and Barnes's own interest in more subtle correspondences in the reality of Christopher's life. In words that intimate many aspects to the quasi-allegorical millennialism of *England, England* and the historiographic metafiction of *A History of the World in 10½ Chapters*, Scholes includes 'modern allegory and 'the range of metafiction' in his review of the approaches of fabulators, saying they 'challenge the notion that history may be retrieved by objective investigations of fact' and find history 'readily adaptable to the artifices of daydream and fabulation'.[19] I have already mentioned that Barnes is a perennially ironic and comic writer, even as we will see in such a modern political fable as *The Porcupine*, and Scholes also considers fabulation's interest in comedy and grotesquerie, pointing us towards the black humour of *Before She Met Me*. Additionally however Scholes affirms in *Fabulation and Metafiction* the range of 'experimental fiction' in ways that exemplify Barnes's inventive and ludic approach to the novel, from the philosophical ideas animating *Staring at the Sun* to the choreographed polyphony of *Talking It Over*. It is also clear that *Flaubert's Parrot* and *Arthur & George*, though in many respects formally different, are texts deeply concerned with how belief, conviction, and desire can shape an understanding of future, past, and present reality. Scholes says that for the fabulator the writer's aim is to 'reach beyond reality to truth' and this is a sentiment about art repeatedly expressed by Barnes, most explicitly in his memoir *Nothing to Be Frightened of*. Reminding the reader of what is perhaps Barnes's dominant literary aspect, Scholes affirms that 'A sense of pleasure in form is one characteristic of fabulation'.[20]

Barnes has said that with each novel he aims to write not just fiction that seems fresh to him but fiction which reinvents the novel itself. This is the element of fabulation that comes through the novels he has written under his own name, characterised by inventiveness, and a scepticism towards concepts like truth, history, and reality. There is also a tendency towards the instructive and the satirical in the way that his fiction, if not always urgent, is none the less provocative and to some extent didactic but always laced with self-reflective scepticism, irony, and wit (provocative but elegantly phrased opinions such as that the purpose of catastrophe is to produce art (HW, p. 125) earned him Mark Lawson's tag as 'the teacher of your dreams').[21] Barnes's more conservative impulses toward realism and reportage have been

channelled into non-fiction and the Duffy novels, which by comparison rely straightforwardly on plot, dialogue, verisimilitude, and
clear chronology, as critics have noted.[22]

Reflecting his commitment to Flaubertian truth and his awareness
of the perils of reinventing the novel, Barnes's characters at times do
comment on literary modes. 'Realism is our given, our only mode,
triste truth as it might come to some' says Oliver (LE, 156), making
an observation as a writer on life's difference from fiction. It is also
true that the narrator of *Flaubert's Parrot*, Geoffrey Braithwaite, notes
how 'We no longer believe that language and reality "match up" so
congruently' (FP, p. 88) but, as the critic Gregory Rubinson observes
of *Flaubert's Parrot*, 'This multi-genre, multi-perspective view of
Flaubert does not necessarily mean that we must abandon historical
inquiry to relativism'.[23] The trajectory of Barnes's writing is far more
towards the admixture of generic approaches to an underlying 'pure
story' rooted in but growing away from the ungraspable realism of
life, whether Flaubert's or Braithwaite's, combined with an understanding that 'you can't define yourself directly, just by looking face-
on in the mirror' (FP, p. 95).

If Barnes's fiction, Mira Stout observes, 'essentially addresses the
spiritual void of the middle-class man'[24] it does so through characters who as Matthew Pateman says 'are striving for some way of finding
meaning in an increasingly depoliticised, secularised, localised and
depthless world'.[25] While Frederick Holmes sees Barnes's concerns
as broadly 'epistemological and ethical',[26] Pateman concurs with
Stout when he conjectures that Barnes's major concern is 'the loss
of faith'.[27] However, he goes on to note helpfully that other central
issues for Barnes are the simultaneous scrutiny of and fear for the
lack of efficacy of myriad grand narratives: art, religion, the promise
of science and technology, the claims of politics, history, the self, and
'the practical effect of love' (Pateman, pp. 84–5). I might add other
aspects of personal and social identity to this list, including memory
and nationality, and observe that Barnes places great stock in such
fairly reliable pleasures as food and friendship (as well as smoking and sex) without descending into Epicureanism from the mix
of pragmatism, stoicism, sceptisim, aestheticism and existential-
ism that underpin much of his worldview. Pateman also observes
that Barnes's fiction oscillates between 'domestic concerns' and
'the lack of myth in the contemporary world'.[28] For my part I see
his work as a balance of moral comedy and sceptical nostalgia in

portraits of a fallen human condition (his opening phrase of *Nothing to Be Frightened of*, 'I don't believe in God but I miss him' (NF, p. 1), would, with small inflections, seem to express Barnes's view of many things). As Holmes concludes, Barnes's fiction 'displays a self-reflexive postmodernist scepticism regarding any truth claims, even those which potentially could anchor personal identity and counter the simulacra of cyber culture'.[29] Highmindedness, melancholy, the illusion of free will and the pursuit of truth, love and art are all displayed barely and ironically. There are no good, brave causes left, as John Osborne's Jimmy Porter opined in *Look Back in Anger*, but there are also no cultural or existential footholds that will support the weight of modern desires for belief, myth, or truth.

Barnes said in discussion with Rudolf Freiburg that 'Shakespeare is nothing if not a mixer of genres, and a mixer of forms of rhetoric, and a mixer of prose and poetry, and a mixer of high and low, and a mixer of farce and tragedy'.[30] Holmes consequently notes Barnes's 'generic mongrelism',[31] and this is the defining feature of his fabulations which mix forms to create unique versions of reality. Barnes's works are formidably intertextual, citing novels, poems, art works, musical compositions, performances, and other cultural artefacts, yet Barnes dislikes his novels being pigeonholed as literary fiction and there is a strong sense of modern life and formal sophistication in his work, but it is also true there appears more historical than contemporary cultural reference.

Though he here refers to Shakespeare, Barnes's experimentation draws more parallels with European or Latin American fiction. 'Style does arise from subject matter' says Braithwaite in deference to Flaubert (see FP, p. 95). Style, the proper 'marriage of content and form', is a cardinal starting-point for Barnes's work which deploys the irony of Flaubertian free indirect discourse and the attention to individual words that characterised Flaubert's refinement of realism into a nascent modernism. This shines in Barnes's work from the poetic linguistic attention of his writings to their unusual and illuminating use of metaphor. His display of epigram and aphorism distinguish him among contemporary British writers where rhetorical devices of a different kind are commonly used. This is central to what makes Barnes distinctive and connects him to a literary tradition that seeks not only to show the world but to describe it insightfully and precisely in original language. This is not an aspiration to objective truth but to observational truth which ascribes viewpoints to characters (including himself in the half-chapter 'Parenthesis' in *History of the World*) and carefully illustrates that parallactic understanding of reality through appropriate images, from the 'Asian times' of Jean Serjeant in *Staring at the Sun*, or the jigsaw nation of Martha Cochrane in *England, England* to the 'weather men' of Stuart in *Talking It Over*. The titles of Barnes's books are often both metonymic and metaphoric: *Flaubert's Parrot*, *Metroland*, and *The Lemon Table*, for example, denote an animal, a place and an object but more than this they stand for aspects of history, identity, and mortality that resonate deeply with the understanding of language associated with modernism rather than with realism (cf. *David Copperfield*, *Middlemarch*, or *North and South*). *Staring at the Sun* and *Cross Channel* are titles in the vein of *Heart of Darkness* or *To the Lighthouse*, with only *Arthur & George* – an early twenty-first century novel about the early twentieth – settling on a comparatively straightforward referential title (the title is appropriate for its historical positioning but was not Barnes's choice).

Barnes has published several non-fiction volumes since the mid-1990s. The first was *Letters from London: 1990–5* (1995), a collection of the *New Yorker* columns he wrote under the guise of a foreign correspondent in his own country. Relishing the role of journalist, Barnes anatomises three British Prime Minsters (Margaret Thatcher, John Major, and Tony Blair as PM-in-waiting) and much of the book focuses on the intrigues, pomposity, and farce of politics, but in these epistolary essays he also ranges over transport, the City, chess, and TV. Barnes gives one account of himself campaigning with the actress turned Labour Party Member of Parliament Glenda Jackson and another of reading the memoirs of the Conservative Prime Minister Thatcher, whom he characterises as running the country like a parade-ground sergeant-major (LL, p. 241). The book covers a variety of English subjects from the royal family to the Rushdie fatwa and it is hard not to see it as contributing to the thoughts that would issue in *England, England* in 1999. One essay, 'Fake!', uses as a title the word he decided not to employ in that novel, but hinges on the precepts 'fakery follows wherever money leads' and, in a Robin Hood image, 'the gap between creative output and market demand is met by a merry band of fakers' (LL, 22).

Barnes has also written a collection of essays on Francophone literature and culture that resulted from journalistic assignments, *Something to Declare* (2002). The second half of the book is devoted to Flaubert but earlier chapters discuss French culture across a range of subjects, considering at some length Georges Simenon, Jacques Brel, François Truffaut, the Tour de France, and Elizabeth David's championing of French cuisine.

Looking again across La Manche, he has additionally edited and translated Alphonse Daudet's *In the Land of Pain*, which is a stoical and at times comical memoir of the nineteenth-century novelist's eventual descent into paralysis following the contraction of syphilis as a teenager. As *Letters from London* fed into *England, England*, and *Something to Declare* is reminiscent at times of subjects covered in *Cross Channel* (1996), Barnes's work on this book lent itself to the thoughts that were to inform both *The Lemon Table* (2004) and *Nothing to Be Frightened of* (2008), which is to a small degree Barnes's non-fictional companion piece to his second collection of short stories.

More recently Barnes has concocted a series of culinary essays on his attempts to follow recipes, called *The Pedant in the Kitchen*, and he has also written the prefaces or introductions to several works by other authors, ranging from Clive James's *Reliable Essays* to Aristotle's *The Nicomachean Ethics*. He has a startling range of interests that span across culture and public life, and this is reflected in the variety of his fictional subjects – Barnes gave up the *Duffy* novels partly because of the constraint that a consistent central character imposed. His writing is witty, urbane, and erudite but there is a consistent celebration of the ordinary that reveals a good deal about his background and upbringing. Such concern with the unexceptional also epitomises the simple values that his books often advocate beneath their sophistication: love, friendship, truth, and courage. None of these is remotely straightforward in Barnes's novels but there is a loyalty to such 'domestic concerns' that suggests the values to which the writer adheres. His first novel *Metroland* (1980) is a rich three-part analysis of emotional growing pains in the suburbs while *Before She Met Me* (1982) is a study of uxoriousness just as much as jealousy in an otherwise unremarkable marriage. *Flaubert's Parrot* (1984) inasmuch as it is Braithwaite's story is a poignant study of loss and displacement completing a trilogy of novels that could be said to focus on common preoccupations of youth and middle age, both early and late, married and bereaved. They are studies of male preoccupations for the most part, and that makes *Staring at the Sun* (1986) all the more remarkable a departure. Another pointed study of ordinary life, it is an examination of the virtue of courage that is extraordinary. This is clear at the very least to the extent that while, Barnes says, people 'tend to think of courage as a male virtue . . . there are 85,000 other sorts of courage' and Jean Serjeant's is an 'ordinary miracle' (SS, p. 4) in an exercise in what Barnes has called 'DIY theology'.[32]

A History of the World in 10 1/2 Chapters (1989) also aims to insinu- ate more of the ordinary and the exceptional into each other's orbit. From the opening story, told from the position of an animal stow- away, to the final summation of an average life in 'The Dream' the book focuses on people whom history would seldom highlight but who illustrate its processes and vagaries: Lawrence Beesley, Miss Fergusson, and Kath Ferris, in whose story, Vanessa Guignery notes, 'Fable and fabulation are cathartic as they attenuate the horror, bru- tality and arbitrariness of the history of the world'.[33] Barnes's love- triangle novels Talking It Over (1991) and Love, etc (2001) delineate three undistinguished interlinked lives, once more adhering to a fictional preoccupation with the ordinary over, for example, journal- ism's almost exclusive focus on the extraordinary. The Porcupine (1992) might seem an exception to the trend I am describing but its spotlight is precisely on a post-Soviet satellite country that Euro- American press coverage had little touched. England, England (1998) counterposes the pomp of Sir Jack Pitman's service-sector magnate with Martha Cochrane's everyday scepticism in a juxtaposition that anticipates Barnes's interest in his next novel in the dynamic between the converging stories of Arthur Conan Doyle and George Edalji. Arthur & George (2005) also signals another convergence. The ludic experimentation and generic polyphony that has marked Barnes's most celebrated fictions, Flaubert's Parrot, A History of the World in 10 1/2 Chapters, and to a lesser extent England, England, is in those novels not matched by a depth to the stories of Geoffrey Braithwaite, Martha Cochrane, or any single figure from A History of the World. However, experimental techniques are successfully blended with a sustained narrative in Arthur & George, which is one of Barnes's most satisfying novels to date in that it combines an extended realist approach with a thematic coherence and an ironic narratorial voice that is less directing than in some earlier works. It also seems to bring together the experimental style with aspects of the writing used in such novels as Staring at the Sun, The Porcupine, and Before She Met Me, which for many critics represent a less analy- tically fruitful side to Barnes's fiction.

I have noted elsewhere that 'Barnes is sometimes considered a post- modernist writer because his fiction rarely either conforms to the model of the realist novel or concerns itself with a scrutiny of consciousness in the manner of modernist writing',[34] and this is a mark both of his diverse influences and of the difficulties of classifying his eclectic fictions. In this study, the books are treated text by text partly because Barnes is clear that he regards each work as a fresh departure and does not think there are continuities that, for example, link his novels together into an oeuvre. Yet, there are preoccupations that appear across the fiction and represent recurrent thematic concerns, including memory, history, representation, belief, truth, art, identity, and death. There are also aspects to the subject matter such as love and adultery that intimate a deep concern with the private and domestic sphere, though this is balanced with a curiosity about the machinations of the public and political worlds in *The Porcupine, Letters from London*, and elsewhere. Aside from Barnes's first novel, his fiction does not have a strong autobiographical element, but there is a significant if not clear-cut moral element to the novels that places Barnes more in a humanist than a postmodernist writing tradition. The insertion of a kind of soliloquy by the author in the 'Parenthesis' chapter of *A History of the World* may add to that novel's sense of eclectic styles and voices but the approach taken is that of a direct address to the reader about the author's opinion: 'every so often you think . . . I'll just write the truth'.[35] This illustrates the way in which Barnes's overriding perspective undermines many uncomplicated discussions of his position as a postmodernist writer, when values of truth, art, and love are so regularly discussed and affirmed in his fiction, even though their efficacy is simultaneously questioned. The form and eclectic approaches of Barnes's fiction thus illustrate the stance of a fabulist who mixes genres and ideas, but his writing is rooted in a set of literary precedents that couch his experimentations in a tradition of formal and self-reflexive invention that looks to the authors he himself references in his work, rather than postmodernist contemporaries. As such his fiction can perhaps best be placed in the 'sceptical, pragmatic, realist, untheoretical strand' of writing that I mentioned near the start of this Introduction and which he himself most favours, though his novels seek nearly always to take this strand in a new, formally experimental direction.

Notes

1 Julian Barnes, 'You ask the questions', *The Independent*, Wednesday Review, 16 January 2002, p. 8.

2 Ibid.

3 One list of Barnes's favourite books is *Madame Bovary* (Flaubert), *Don Juan* (Byron), *Persuasion* (Austen), *Anna Karenina* (Tolstoy), *Candide* (Voltaire), *The Custom of the Country* (Wharton), *The Good Soldier* (Ford), *The Leopard* (di Lampedusa), *Rabbit Angstrom: The Four Novels* (Updike), *Amours de Voyage* (Clough). See J. Peder Zane, *The Top Ten: Writers Pick Their Favorite Books*, New York: Norton, 2007, p. 39. Barnes has written introductions to several of these texts, including those by Ford and Clough.

4 Mike French Interview with Julian Barnes, *The View From Here* magazine, www.viewfromheremagazine.com/2008/04/mike-interviews-julian-barnes-part-3-of.html (accessed 6 November 2009).

5 Mira Stout, 'Chameleon novelist', *The New York Times Magazine*, 22 November 1992, Section 6, p. 68.

6 Richard Bradford, *The Novel Now*, Oxford: Blackwell, 2007, p. 48.

7 Frederick M. Holmes, *Julian Barnes*, London: Palgrave, 2009, p. 27.

8 Matthew Pateman, *Julian Barnes*, Plymouth: Northcote House, 2002, p. 3.

9 Brian Moore, *I am Mary Dunne*, London: Flamingo, 1995, p. 1.

10 Vanessa Guignery, '"History in question(s)": an interview with Julian Barnes', reprinted in Vanessa Guignery and Ryan Roberts (eds), *Conversations with Julian Barnes*, Jackson: University Press of Mississippi, 2009, p. 63.

11 Barnes: 'You ask the questions', p. 8.

12 Guignery, '"History in question(s)": an interview with Julian Barnes', pp. 54–5.

13 David Lodge, *The Novelist at the Crossroads*, London: Routledge, 1971, p. 4.

14 Ibid., p. 22.

15 'The art of fiction CLXV', Shusha Guppy's interview with Barnes, reprinted in Guignery and Roberts, *Conversations with Julian Barnes*, p. 66.

16 This book is a revised version of *The Fabulators*.

17 Robert Scholes, *Fabulation and Metafiction*, Urbana: University of Illinois Press, 1979, p. 4.

18 Ibid., p. 8.

19 Ibid., pp. 206–7.

20 Ibid., p. 2.

21 Mark Lawson, 'A short history of Julian Barnes', *Independent* Magazine, 13 July 1991, pp. 34–6, p. 34.

22 See the discussion in Vanessa Guignery, *The Fiction of Julian Barnes*, London: Palgrave, 2006, p. 32.

23 Gregory J. Rubinson, *The Fiction of Rushdie, Barnes, Winterson, and Carter: Breaking Cultural and Literary Bounds in the Work of Four Postmodernists*, Jefferson, NC: McFarland, 2005, p. 84.

24 Stout, 'Chameleon novelist', p. 72.

25 Pateman, *Julian Barnes*, p. 2.

26 Holmes, *Julian Barnes*, p. 24.
27 See Peter Childs, 'Beneath a bombers' moon: Barnes and belief' in Vanessa Guignery (ed.), *Worlds within Words: Twenty-first Century Visions on the Work of Julian Barnes*, Special issue of *The Journal of American, British and Canadian Studies* 13 (December 2009).
28 Pateman, *Julian Barnes*, p. 84.
29 Holmes, *Julian Barnes*, pp. 12–13.
30 Barnes to Rudolf Freiburg in his interview 'Novels come out of life not out of theories', reprinted in Guignery and Roberts, *Conversations with Julian Barnes*, p. 47.
31 Holmes, *Julian Barnes*, p. 15.
32 Quotations taken from Merritt Moseley, 'Julian Barnes' in Merritt Moseley (ed.), *Dictionary of Literary Biography: British Novelists Since 1960*, Second Series, Volume 194, Detroit: Gale, 1998, p. 34.
33 Guignery, *The Fiction of Julian Barnes*, p. 67.
34 Peter Childs, *Contemporary Novelists: British Fiction Since 1970*, London: Macmillan, 2005, p. 86.
35 Alexander Stuart, 'A talk with Julian Barnes', *Los Angeles Times*, 15 October 1989: http://articles.latimes.com/1989-10-15/books/bk-163_1_julian-barnes (accessed 6 November 2009).

1

About to be less deceived: *Metroland*

Verlaine's brother-in-law described Rimbaud [aged 17 when he met Verlaine] as 'a vile, vicious, disgusting, smutty little schoolboy', but Verlaine found him an 'exquisite creature'.[1]

One of the few unsurprising steps that Barnes has taken in his literary career concerns the subject of his first novel. This is alluded to in *Flaubert's Parrot*, whose narrator advocates 'A partial ban on growing-up novels (one per author allowed)' (FP, p. 99). In a long-established tradition, and after many years of drafting and honing, Barnes produced a debut that inclined towards the autobiographical and focused upon the evolution of one suburban schoolboy's artistic temperament alongside his significant life-experiences, from adolescence through to young adulthood and parenthood.

However, written self-consciously in the shadow of numerous 'first novels', *Bildungsromans*, and French cultural touchstones from Alain-Fournier's 1913 novel *Le Grand Meaulnes* to François Truffaut's 1962 film *Jules et Jim*, Barnes's debut is a contemplative and reflective fictional memoir that affirms the value of simple pleasures and resists the Larkinesque temptation to believe that 'life' lies somewhere else: beyond suburbia, at political riots and protests, or in leading a Bohemian existence. The story is told by the protagonist Christopher Lloyd, looking back on periods of his life, borrowing some of the texture and geography of Barnes's own youth. The retrospective narration, common to first-person novels such as *Great Expectations* and *Jane Eyre*, is primarily apparent through small asides ('To this day, I have a preference for sleeping on my left side', M, p. 54) rather than any direct commentary by Christopher on his younger self. The book's narrator thus appears to be Christopher on the day after the book's final scene ('Last night, Amy woke . . .', M, p. 175) but this is not explicitly stated. The narrative moves gently and unsentimentally towards its conclusion that, caught between the unexciting but satis-fying domesticity he has with Marion and the superficially attractive but ultimately hollow hedonism of schoolmate Toni, Christopher has matured into what he considers life-learned 'happiness'. Meanwhile his emotionally arrested friend has sought to remain true to the spirit of his schoolboy self and ideals at the expense of adult responsibili-ties or a capacity for either life-enabling adaptation or reflective self-awareness. Toni continues to live without a sense of compromise, while Christopher perceives happiness to reside in fitting in with society and with the shape of others' lives, establishing a niche rather than a stance of rebellion.[2]

That adolescent identity, to whose principles Toni wishes to remain narrowly true, is first sketched in the novel's opening pages. In 1963, two 16-year-old schoolboys at the City of London School on the Embankment look for signs of the effect and affect art produces in the observer. They make notes, hoping to discern and record the visible traces of quasi-religious experiences in visitors to the National Gallery in Trafalgar Square. Sounding a note that will resound through Barnes's works, Christopher's appreciation of art also has a deep root in his fear of death: 'Belief in art was initially an effective simple against the routine ache of big D' (M, p. 55). At home he is caught between a sister, Mary, who is too sensitive, and a brother, Nigel, who is insensitive to Christopher's fears of death. The rest of his family figure only little, though Christopher's relationship with his Uncle Arthur provides a comical education in truth and lies, which is to be repeated in Jean Serjeant's relationship with her uncle in *Staring at the Sun*.

Christopher and Toni make art, music, and literature the focus of their lives' interest, leaning towards all things French and assessing potential heroes on the basis of how much they advocate bohemian living and despise the bourgeoisie's placid domesticity. To the two boys everything also contains 'more symbolism' (M, p. 13) than other and ordinary people realise. Their belief, embedded in late-nineteenth-century aesthetics, is that life is open to meaning, interpretation, and correspondences, provided it is studied closely enough. A woman's reaction to a Van Dyck painting suggests to them she 'scented new correspondences' (M, p. 12) in the painting, making her a symbolist if only she knew it. The boys conduct similar aesthetic experiments on themselves when listening to music, seeking to document the civilising force of exposure to artistic excellence. Their thoughts are hemmed in by the large abstractions they idolise, elevating but also reifying their lives in terms of a search for truth, art, love, language, self, and, ironically, authenticity.

As is common in his writings, Barnes works with a three-part structure in *Metroland*, but there is little sense of dialectic movement from thesis through antithesis to synthesis; instead Barnes shapes a there-and-back-again traveller's tale which suggests Eliot's famous lines on the end of exploring in 'Little Gidding': 'to arrive where we started / And know the place for the first time.' The Parts follow Christopher's life from 16 to 30, each phase expressing his current attitude to the relationship between art and life. In Part One, he and Toni believe in the Decadent aesthete's mantra of 'art for art's sake' and have no life to speak of in the sense of any degree of independence, self-determination, or responsibility. Unaligned with others but still situated in the burgeoning principles of youthful rebellion, they are ensconced in 1963, the year in which Philip Larkin said in his poem 'Annus Mirabilis' that sex began; but they are rootless in terms of the practicalities of life. Reference to Larkin is made when Toni and Chris discuss, in the terms of Larkin's poem 'This Be the Verse', how parents 'fug you up' but 'were fugged up in their turn' (M, p. 39). The poem itself was not written until 1971 and so the reference is retrospective on the part of either Christopher or Barnes, but the spirit of Larkin's 1955 collection *The Less Deceived* permeates the darker aspects of the novel in its emphasis on a dread of death, the state of Englishness, and the waning of affect. Toni and Chris see themselves as part of the postwar 'Anger generation' contemporary with Larkin but infused with the existential angst of Camus and the alienation of his character Meursault from *L'Étranger*: 'independent existence could only be achieved by strict deconditioning.' (M, p. 41) While Toni's parents are religious, disciplinarian, loving, and poor, Chris's are, he believes, simply dull: his parents' outlook and morality are to be rejected and reversed, his siblings both have 'bland, soft-featured, unresentful faces', and all the family live what Chris perceives to be an unendurably empty existence (M, pp. 40–2). Chris is located squarely in Metroland while Toni is an inner-city child, but they are united in their hatred of 'unidentified legislators, moralists, social luminaries and parents' (M, p. 14) while they themselves ponder Love, Truth, Authenticity, and 'the purity of the language, the perfectibility of self, the function of art' (M, p. 15).

A single spoken word begins Chapter 5 of the novel's first Part: 'Rootless'. Barnes says: 'I grew up in a place that looks like a settled community but is in fact full of rootless people. You have this psychic rootlessness which is characteristic of who we are.'[3] That Metroland is a commuter zone underlines this point when Christopher finds travelling between identities replaces a unified sense of self with a 'twice-daily metamorphosis' (M, 58). He travels from his home identity, house-trained adolescent, to his school identity, anti-social *flâneur*, donning and doffing his feelings of teenage inexperience or his affectations as a post-industrial Rimbaudian aesthete. Art appears a form of compensation for the necessity of vicarious living, as well as a consolation for mortality. Another compensation in this closely structured three-part commuter novel, where Paris more than London is in fact both the metaphorical and the literal destination before Chris's return to Metroland, is travel. In the rootlessness of Chapter 5, and anticipating the end of the story that concludes *Cross Channel*, 'Tunnel', Christopher encounters a middle-aged gentleman travelling on his train. The man explains something of the history of the rail lines that run through Metroland, situating Christopher's recent understanding in the context of Victorian expansion and ambition, lionising the very society that Chris's heroes spurn: 'He was an old sod, I thought; dead bourgeois' (M, p. 35). Chris's preference for art over life reveals itself again in his ignorant dismissal of the Victorian railway pioneer Sir Edward Watkin merely as someone 'who couldn't tell Tissot from Titian' (M, p. 37). Watkin's grand idea of connecting the northern English cities to the Continent using one vast railway line is contrasted with Chris's parochial, unambitious mental and physical Metroland, which the old man dismisses as 'nonsense . . . Cosy homes for cosy heroes. Twenty-five minutes from Baker Street and a pension at the end of the line . . . a bourgeois dormitory' (M, p. 38). The man's self-recognition as a bourgeois himself puzzles Chris, who is at present unable to reconcile the often different aspirations of art and life or to appreciate that an individual's choice of life's responsibilities over art's priorities might be defensible, let alone condonable. This attitude of art-inspired rebellion he terms 'Scorched Earth': 'systematic rejection, wilful contradiction, a wide-ranging, anarchic slate-wipe' (M, p. 41).[4] Yet, it is central to the narrative that this rejection of values is aesthetic not anarchic, unmatched in Christopher by any strong political motivation, which in many ways marks his split from the increasingly radical Toni and his own segue into leftist liberalism.

The lack of historical recognition in particular highlights this aspect of Chris's life. Across the carefully dated three parts, the impact of the Beatles in 1963, the student protests in Paris in 1968, and the Punk movement in 1977 are all overlooked by Christopher at the time, with only the middle one acknowledged at all by his solipsistic narrative. Even in the first part, Christopher is largely indifferent to politics because he agrees with Osborne's Jimmy Porter that there are no brave causes left. He tells Toni that they are of course part of the Anger Generation and that the fact they are studying John Osborne's work at school means they are being institutionalised: 'heading off the revolt of the intelligentsia by trying to absorb it into the body politic' (M, p. 41). This apparent awareness of Marxist thought is then undermined by Chris's paradoxical joke that 'maybe the real action's in Complacency' (ibid.), whereas Toni at least has stronger revolutionary potential because he has stricter parents than Chris. Most clear here is in fact the importance of not action but language and rhetoric in the boys' self-development.

Part One's epigraph reads: 'A noir, E blanc, I rouge, U vert, O bleu'. It is taken from Rimbaud's sonnet 'Voyelles' ('Vowels', 1871), a poem that builds on his hero Baudelaire's poem 'Correspondences' (1857). In intellectual terms a precursor to structuralism, Rimbaud's poem creates a link between vowels and colours that emphasises synaesthetic correspondences, putatively connecting objects and the individual's private world. A key importance of this to *Metroland* is that Barnes's novel records one adolescent's rendering of the world through his own imaginative equations between life and art. Christopher and Toni are so appalled by the disjunction between life and art that they try to observe any influence that the latter has on the former. Their activity tries in the simplest way to make manifest the belief not only that art civilises but also that there is a correspondence between the art observed and the observer that they observe. It is a leisured, adolescent, idealistic, and naive enterprise that characterises their lack of experience and their estranged, essentially voyeuristic engagement with life, amounting to a pretentious, but amusingly absurd, equivalent of trainspotting. The boys believe they are 'hunting emotions': aesthetic ones at art galleries, loving ones at railway termini, fearful ones at doctors' surgeries, spiritual ones at church. The National Gallery is their most regular haunt because

> Art was the most important thing in life, the constant to which one could be unfailingly devoted and which would never cease to reward; more crucially, it was the stuff whose effect on those exposed to it was ameliorative. It made people not just fitter for friendship and more civilised (we saw the circularity of *that*), but *better* – kinder, wiser, nicer, more peaceful, more active, more sensitive. If it didn't, what good was it? (M, p. 29)

This last question is one that has itself remained constant in Barnes's writing, with working answers appearing in diverse places from *A History of the World in 10½ Chapters* (art commemorates if not ameliorates catastrophe) to *Nothing to Be Frightened of* (art conveys truths, unlike religion).

The adolescent Chris conjectures that, if individuals are in some way improved when they are exposed to art, the process could be visible. The 30-year-old Chris concludes, by contrast, that life is more important than art. But Barnes's novel implies something in-between may be the case: first, that art leaves an after-image, and, second, that virtues Christopher has as an adult can be partly traced back to his teenage influences. In the story's narrative trajectory, this is the arc of the journey Christopher has been on, when thinking about commuting and grander travels. Talking of his suitcase, he says at the end of Part One that 'One day I shall fix the real labels on myself'; and this is what has happened by the end of the novel, as he has moved from 'mentally stick[ing] labels' to being labelled himself. The suitcase is one of the key objects of Chris's adolescence, informing his still unformed sense of self.

The final chapter of each Part of Barnes's book is entitled 'Object Relations'. At the close of Part One this chapter locates the juvenile Christopher's memories and awareness of self in the objects that surround him in his bedroom: 'I remember things' (M, p. 71) is his own response to his question about first and strongest adolescent memories. The confines and contents of his room are 'objects redolent of all I felt and hoped for'. Also, 'The whole room is full of things I don't have' (M, p. 72), exposing his sense of both expectation and frustration. This is partly because these badges of identity are not necessarily selected by him: 'Is that so strange? What else are you at that age but a creature part willing, part consenting, part being chosen?' (M, 72). In such places, the interstices of the novel, Barnes allows the older Christopher less to judge than to understand his younger self, making sense of his relationship to his own past.

The epigraph to Part Two of the novel answers back to the epigraph of Part One quoted above. It is a comment from Verlaine on the extract from Rimbaud's poem: 'Moi qui ai connu Rimbaud, je sais qu'il se foutait pas mal si A était rouge ou vert. Il le voyait comme ça, mais c'est tout' ('I who knew Rimbaud, know that he really didn't give a damn whether A was red or green. He saw it like that, but that's all'). The suggestion here is that a personal expression or vision should not be mistaken for an objective correlative.

'Rimbaud's "Voyelles",' says Barnes, 'is about how you see life at 18. The Verlaine quote is about how realism kicks in.'[5] This is clearly played out in the novel. Indeed, Chris and Toni acknowledge, 'Life didn't really get under way until you left school' (M, p. 42), justifying the reflex response of their Scorched Earth policy as the first stage of a two-part process that will give way to 'Reconstruction' in stage two, when they will have choices, relationships, and the burden of moral decisions. In Part Two, Christopher thus attempts at 21 to make art and life compatible in 1968 by realising his dream of a garret-room Parisian life. Barnes locates this Part in the key year of youthful rebellion but has Christopher holed up in a love-nest, almost entirely oblivious to the challenges being made to traditional authority around him. 'But I didn't actually see anything' says Christopher, who explains in a letter to Toni that the rioting students of les événements were simply frustrated at not being able to understand their courses.

At 21, after his first degree, Christopher is researching a postgraduate thesis in Paris. 'I went to Paris determined to immerse myself in the culture, the language, the street-life, and . . . the women' (M, p. 105). Here, in a large but familiar city he begins to fancy himself 'as an autonomous being' (M, p. 85). His research is secondary to his attempt to integrate life and art in acting out the principles of his adolescence. For example, he develops the Constructive Loaf, in which he and Toni used to indulge, into the Haphazard Principle of catching life on the hop by suddenly drawing a picture of a randomly chosen moment of being.

Chris is impressed by the cultural experience of a long-imagined and protracted stay in Paris; particularly by the fact that 'bringing it all together, ingesting it, making it mine, was me – fusing all the art and the history with what I might soon, with luck, be calling the life'.

(M, p. 93) A fusion of life and art is what he imagines is happening when he starts going out with a French girl, Annick, but Barnes more often juxtaposes the two, and in any case Christopher's sense of both art and history are somewhat arrested, with little sense they are happening in the here and now as well as the past.

Chris is also still a virgin, sexually fascinated but inexperienced. He has had sexual opportunities but only one real relationship, an unconsummated couple of months with a girl called Janet, the local solicitor's daughter. As Chris's life develops new dimensions his relationship with Toni fades into the background, their epistolary correspondence throwing up fresh differences of opinion, which seem to hang off themes of love and sex more than hinge on their other childhood passions: 'The enemies who had given us common cause were no longer there; our adult enthusiasms were bound to be less congruent than our adolescent hates' (M, p. 97). Chris learns new attitudes from Annick: that truth needn't be arrived at by combat; that there is value in honesty of response but also of expression. Chris starts to reflect and mature in ways that begin to take him away from a world built on intellectual snobbery, assumed superiority, and scorn for the lives of others.

Somewhat ironically, in Paris he falls into the company of three English people he meets at an art gallery. One of these is Marion, with whom he begins another relationship. What his relationships with Annick and Marion teach Chris is that he has not been paying attention to life. Annick explains that he learns melodramatically through instruction while she learns quietly through observation (M, p. 102). Similarly with Marion, Chris accuses her of reading La Rochefoucauld to arrive at her opinions, but she replies that she has come to her conclusions though a study of life: 'I've been observing' (M, p. 116). Chris, with Toni, has previously focussed only on observing the effects of art on life, unconcerned and possibly unaware that life may be observed itself. ' "Some people say that life is the thing, but I prefer reading": we would have endorsed that guiltily at the time, guilty because we feared that our passion for art was the result of the emptiness of our "lives" ' (M, p. 128).

As he departs Paris, Christopher's questions now are about the connection, balance, and interaction of life and art. Looking once more around a room, this time the apartment he is leaving, he decides 'The final object was me. Packed tight like my suitcase – I'd had to sit on top of me to get it all in. The moral and sensual equivalents of theatre programmes were all there' (M, p. 130). He leaves Paris with a knowing copy of Flaubert's *L'Éducation Sentimentale* in his pocket and with experiences of living to process alongside his reading.

The Third Part's epigraph signals the next turn in Christopher's life. It is from the sermons of Joseph Butler, Bishop of Durham (1692–1752): 'Things and actions are what they are, and the conse-quences of them will be what they will be; why then should we desire to be deceived?' (*Fifteen Sermons*, VII). The quotation implies that a period of English pragmatism will be succeeding two blasts of Gallic abstraction in Parts One and Two. Part Three sees Christopher apparently abandoning art and conforming to the suburban values he despised as a teenager because they bring him happiness and shape his identity, while art has less meaning for his adult life in Metroland.

The book thus completes its movement from all art and no life, though an attempt at having it all in Paris, to an adult life without the romance of Paris or the childhood ideals about art to which his friend Toni still clings, albeit in a contemporary, politicised form. 'I suppose I must be grown-up now' (M, p. 133) starts Part Three with an ambiguity of expression that allows both a reading of hesitant uncer-tainty and also one of resigned determination. On the one hand, this is a conjecture on his social evolution: Christopher has reached an age of psychical maturity and has a job as an editor. On the other hand, he feels he has to act like an 'adult' because he has responsi-bilities such as a family and a mortgage. But it is also because he feels he is moving on from theories about life to the act of living (M, p. 135). He has given up 'deviousness', 'half-truths' and 'meta-communication' as 'wonderful in theory, but unreliable in practice' (M, p. 140). Toni blames the world for not allowing art to matter while Chris agrees with the modern bottom-line of Auden's statement that '*poetry* makes nothing happen' (M, p. 145). Chris thinks instead that he is 'into life', but qualifies this by saying in fact that he is simply being 'more serious', as opposed to being intense as a schoolboy or being a bohemian in Paris.

Toni, by contrast, wishes still to live by theories, as he explains: 'Do you remember, when we were at school, when life had a capital letter and it was all Out There somehow, we used to think that the way to live our lives was to discover or deduce certain principles from which individual decisions could be worked out?' (M, p. 150). To Toni, Chris is now living on hunches rather than worked-out principles of behaviour. However, the next step in Chris's sentimental education occurs at a party when he flirts with a girl and is surprised to find that she expects him to have sex with her. He is shocked and counters that he has behaved acceptably when she accuses him of dishonesty. After lessons of response, expression, and observation taught to him by Annick and Marion in Paris, he is now taught about 'honesty of intention' (M, p. 155) by a third woman. When confessing this scene later at home he also learns of Marion's infidelity and is able to come to terms with that fact that they have common fears of neglect, diminished individuality or self-worth, and sexual overfamiliarity.

While Chris is offered by Toni an example of an anti-bourgeois life in the present, his Uncle Arthur is a character who presents to him an alternative possible future. In Part One we learn of Arthur's bachelor lifestyle and his sparring with Chris, which focuses on Arthur's way of always giving Chris tasks to do on family visits and Chris trying to find ways to get revenge for this imposition. In Part Three, Arthur is still trying to get others to do work for him and uses various tricks to achieve this with Marion and Chris. But when Arthur dies Chris is both struck by the circumstances and abandoned objects of a chosen lonely life and aware that his childhood fear of death has largely passed since he started his own family. In the final scenes of the book, Chris explains to Toni that he has lost his faith in the direct link and deep connection between art and life, and then leaves to attend a school reunion where he is offered a job running a new publishing imprint that will mainly produce translations of French classics. This appears as a compromise, in both senses: as an uncommitted half-measure in Toni's terms but also as a way to feed his literary interest and still to earn his living, combining poetry and responsibility: 'A Noir, E blanc, I rouge . . . ? Pay your bills. That's what Auden said' (M, p. 175).

The third version or iteration of 'Object Relations' appears as the novel's final chapter. Here, the orange sodium light from the street lamp stands as a sign of life that comforts both Christopher and his daughter Amy (M, p. 175). This comfort seems enough for Chris, who feels he need not confront the world but can find a 'lazy pleasure' in domesticity, surrounded by a family's gathered 'Objects' that, through associations and memories, 'contain absent people' (M, p. 176). Like the man he met many years ago on the train, Chris is bourgeois in lifestyle but still aware of his choice: just because he cuts the lawn in stripes on Saturday afternoons, don't think he 'can't still quote Mallarmé' (M, p. 174). The comfortable domestic order suggested by the striped lawn is matched by a mature simplicity and happiness that has replaced his younger self's quest for grandiloquent earnestness and angst.

Christopher's volte-face is reflected in the language used at the start and close of the novel, and the book's own artistic correspondences stand as a partly ironic refutation as well as realisation of his position. The woman in the Gallery at the story's start closes her eyes as if 'savouring the after-image' of Van Dyck's painting; Christopher ends the book left with a 'blue-green after-image' of the orange streetlight that has suddenly snapped off, bringing to mind the opening epigraph from Rimbaud. This orange streetlight has also turned the stripe in his pyjamas brown recalling how at the start of the novel he notes how this new orange sodium lighting turns the red colours sported by his mother into dark brown (M, p. 14). This observation is of major significance to Christopher, and even explains his interest in French over English literature: 'How would [Johnson and Yeats] react if all the reds in the world turned to brown? One would hardly notice it has happened; the other would be blinded by the shock' (M, p. 16). This is part of the richly symbolic world of correspondences Christopher inhabited as a teenager and which 'had all started one summer holiday, when I'd taken Baudelaire with me to read on the beach' (M, p. 14). Now, he concludes at the age of 30, 'there's no point in trying to thrust false significances on to things' (M, p. 176). For the reader, however, it is clear that Christopher himself is an after-image of his childhood self: an image that remains in negative after the original light has passed.

In Barnes's notes and drafts of the novel it is clear that by the third section he intends to show that Christopher has experienced a decline in passion: he hasn't confronted the world but can get by without doing so. His younger self sought a stance in the world rather than an authenticity, shown by the adherence to a dogmatic schoolboy argot, with its running words, such as Epat, Ruined, Chippy, syphilised, and fug. In revision Barnes made changes to make the parallels to Part One in Part Three less relentless, giving Marion more of a presence and sharpness, reinforcing her anti-romanticism and self-assurance. In Part Three, Chris is less becoming a smug bourgeois, as Toni would position him, than submitting semi-gracefully to the onset of mature contentment and the recognition of adult realities. These realities are conveyed by his relationship with the

luggage at the end of each Part while his spirit of adventure is channelled into sex, which is presented therefore 'as a form of travel'. Sex
also structures the novel in the way that each part is dominated by
one other character: Toni, then Annick, then Marion. The relations
Chris has with these is in part determined by different attitudes towards
sex, which follow an arc of juvenile prurience through sexual exploration to comfortable but unexciting familiarity. Each of the other
three characters reflects aspects to Chris's development and is in a
way a counterpart to his current sense of self, just as other figures,
from his family members to most incidental characters, stand as foils
who have furthered his moral and sentimental education in the eyes
of the older narrator.

Metroland is written in the shadow of familiar stories of outsider
rebels, epitomised by the legend of Rimbaud and made more relevant
by the contrast between the Betjeman–Larkin image of Metroland and
the riotous presence in London in the previous century of Verlaine
and Rimbaud, not far from the Euston Square stop on Chris's
underground commute along the Metropolitan Line. In 1873, two years
after they met, the French writers were

> living in a house in Camden Town. The terraced house is still there,
> though in a dilapidated state and in an area that can only be described
> as bleak. Beside the front door there is a simple plaque: 'The French
> poets Paul Verlaine and Arthur Rimbaud lived here May–July 1873' . . .
> Rimbaud was 'delighted and astonished' by London. Verlaine was over-
> whelmed by the 'incessant railways on splendid cast-iron bridges' and
> the 'brutal, loud-mouthed people in the streets', but inspired by the 'inter-
> minable['] docks. The city was, he wrote, 'prudish, but with every vice
> on offer', and, 'permanently sozzled, despite ridiculous bills on drunken-
> ness'. The two poets were often sozzled, too: on ale, gin and absinthe.
> Rimbaud's extraordinary sonnet 'Voyelles' (Vowels), which gained an
> instant cult following, was clearly inspired by his experiments with 'the
> Green Fairy'.[6]

But Rimbaud is additionally relevant to Chris's story because of his
early rejection of the artist's life. Rimbaud's later years before his pre-
mature death at the age of 37 were spent travelling (in Europe but
later Indonesia, Java, Cyprus, Yemen, and Ethiopia) and working as
a trader, at first for an overseas agency then independently. After the
age of 20 he gave up writing and turned to a steady working life in
a shift that Christopher's life in some ways parallels.

However, it would be easy to overstate the sense of a positive ending to *Metroland*. The book does not endorse Christopher's position

but instead suggests he has reached an accommodation with what he sees as the reality of his upbringing and circumstances; he is a contented husband and father, but he is also still young and, despite some ambiguity, the novel ends with a reassuring quasi-realist, pre-modernist sense of closure. The contradictions if not necessarily incompatibilities of bohemia and English suburban living lie at the heart of the novel's wry humour, together with the juxtaposition of imaginings inspired by reading conducted in a bored, youthful fervour of longing with the pleasant but unambitious lived reality of a mundane English middle-class existence. This functions in the book in a similar fashion to the double-consciousness used in, for example, Dickens's *Great Expectations*, where two understandings and perspectives are simultaneously presented for the reader to contemplate: 'How does adolescence come back most vividly to you?' (M, p. 71) the older Chris asks, inviting an appreciation of life's changes, its losses and gains: its object relations.

Object relations theory is a branch of psychoanalytic theory that argues for the importance of a dynamic process of psychic development in the subject in relation to others, both real and internalised. 'Object' here therefore refers to significant others, beginning with one's earliest care giver but encompassing other important interpersonal relations. The object is therefore akin to a grammatical position, as in 'Before She Met Me' where 'she' is the 'subject' and the object is 'me'. In *Metroland*, Chris's family and the objects in his bedroom are formative influences, but it is the dynamics of three key personal relationships, with Toni, Annick and Marion, that shape Chris's mental and moral development. Also important however are the internal objects that Chris represents to himself: his bourgeois family, alien siblings, arch-nemesis Uncle Arthur, and the literary figures of his imagination. Though Barnes is not literally using object relations theory, which describes the mental development of children, its principles apply to the tripartite self-modelling, through relationships to real and imagined others, that Christopher moves through. The three Parts document his relations with people while the concluding chapters shift the emphasis to internalised ideas associated with 'Things', the first word of the first 'Object Relations'. In Part One, Chris has his paperbacks of Rimbaud and Baudelaire 'lovingly covered in transparent Fablon . . . so that the Fablon, folded over to a depth of half an inch, covers the decisive capitals of CHRISTOPHER LLOYD' (M, p. 71). In Part Two, 'The final object was me': an object formed through interactions that are crammed into the suitcase

of self and are the 'moral and sensual equivalents of theatre programmes' (M, p. 130). Chris has now embarked on his sentimental
education and instead of poets overwriting his identity he is
crammed full of experiences with others, some the source of shame,
some evidencing 'genuine sensitivity'. In Part Three, which begins
with Toni and ends with Chris's daughter, Amy is the final 'object
relation' that anchors Chris's sense of identity: 'I fear for her when
she cries, and fear for her when she goes quiet' (M, p. 175). Now objects
are avatars: a dozen glasses imply ten friends, and a feeding-bottle
predicts a second baby: 'Objects contain absent people' (M, p. 176),
Chris concludes, underlining the realisation that objects are most
important for their associations with people (M, p. 176). He has
moved from objects that imply writers he doesn't know, through self-
reference, to a life in which objects are the tokens of interpersonal
relations.

Arguably, what *Metroland* best expresses is the fusing in Barnes's
work of French and English sensibilities. The book's title is also
a portmanteau of the French underground, *metro*, with the word
England, and Christopher's Francophilia comes to be tempered,
when he meets Marion, by an English pragmatism that seeps under
his skin: one that for example deflates his ideas about *amour* by
arguing that people perhaps get married for rather more mundane,
practical reasons than deep love and that a belief in grand passions
leading to lifelong cohabitation is 'misplaced idealism'. The implication is that the correspondences Chris wishes to trace between art
and life are also simply 'a determination to prove you're capable
of the ultimate experience' (M, p. 116). That these two characters
subsequently marry exemplifies Christopher's homecoming to
Metroland, with a bourgeois English love of French aesthetics that
will run through Barnes's work, leaving him often seeming somewhat Gallic to his country people but distinctly Anglo-Saxon to those
across the channel.

Notes

1 Christina Patterson, 'Verlaine and Rimbaud: poets from hell', *The
   Independent*, 8 February 2006, www.independent.co.uk/arts-entertainment/
   books/features/verlaine-and-rimbaud-poets-from-hell-525605.html (accessed
   26 March 2009).
2 Matthew Pateman describes Toni's role as representing 'a macho leftism
   that seems redundant and cynical'. Pateman, *Julian Barnes*, p. 5.

3 Stout, 'Chameleon novelist', p. 72.
4 In early drafts the chapter had a counterpart in Part Three where the 30-year-old Chris meets his schoolboy *Doppelgänger* who expresses out loud to Chris all the hostility and prejudice he himself held as a teenager.
5 Patterson, 'Verlaine and Rimbaud'.
6 Ibid.

2

Silly to worry about: *Before She Met Me*

Men were supposed to know, and women were supposed not to mind how they had found out. Jean didn't mind: it was silly to worry about Michael's life before she met him.

Staring at the Sun, p. 40

Barnes's second novel can be read on its own as a darkly comic story of paranoid love leading to violence and self-destruction. However, as a follow-up to *Metroland* it has a context lent to it by the first book and a specific place in Barnes's development as a novelist. Superficially a study in jealousy of Shakespearean proportions, *Before She Met Me* can also be seen as a reactionary novel: an attack on the view that the sexual revolution of the 1960s was uniformly liberating. Its central characters constitute a triad of a kind that will be familiar in Barnes's novels: a woman and two men, as in *Talking It Over, Love, etc*, and the last part of *Metroland*. As in *Metroland*, the central characters are a contented but conventional protagonist (Graham Hendrick, a historian at London University), his less conventional friend (Jack Lupton, novelist), and a woman whose mature attitude to sex contrasts with those of the men (Ann, an ex-actress and Graham's second wife). The main themes of the novel concern the relationship between reason and passion at a particular point in social history, advocating how the 1960s changed sexual manners but not feelings, and emphasising how difficult it can be to control primitive but unwanted emotions.

The action of the novel takes place in 1981 when Graham is 42 and Ann is 35. This is four years after they first met at a party in 1977, when Graham was still married (which may remind the reader of Christopher Lloyd's decision not to commit adultery at a party that same year). Ann at this time had recently stopped working as a minor actress and started a career in fashion. The novel's story centres less on their evolving relationship than on the disintegration of the historian Graham's sanity as he fixates on Ann's past.

In the comic tradition of books by such writers as Kingsley Amis and Angus Wilson, *Before She Met Me*, which Barnes considers his funniest novel, ends with the protagonist Graham brutally killing the close friend who introduced him to his second wife, before himself committing suicide. The story's humour derives from the sardonic wit with which Barnes charts Graham's gradual thought-tormented descent into psychopathological violence from his initial security, conveyed by the book's opening lines: 'The first time Graham Hendrick watched his wife commit adultery he didn't mind at all. He even found himself chuckling' (BS, p. 9).

Rejected early titles for *Before She Met Me* included: 'Wet dreams about the royal family'; 'A sensible man'; 'A reasonable man'; 'Within reason'; 'Reason not the need'; 'Needs must'; and 'Sex in the head'. Others introduced the element of time and suggested the final title: 'A backward glance'; 'Looking backwards'; 'The day Before yesterday'; 'Yesterday's love'; 'Yesterday's men'. The novel's two epigraphs assert pithily that marriage is better than death (Molière)[1] and that the human brain is composed of three differently evolved parts, which are at conflict in terms of their drives and desires and perhaps structurally comparable as a model to Freud's id, ego, and superego. Appropriate to this mental landscape, the book has an enclosed, claustrophobic feel, though this is partly because there are so few characters and a relatively limited number of locations. A play would be quite possible to fashion from the major scenes, which are predominantly interior ones. Barnes sees *Before She Met Me* as the working out of an initial situation as opposed to a mapping of characters, for example. The book is a black comedy that builds from a simple premise to a *psychologically* plausible ending: one which takes Graham's obsession to its logical conclusion rather than adhering to the staples of social realism, whose generic conventions Barnes has never been keen to follow.

However, in terms of its formal qualities, *Before She Met Me* is arguably Barnes's most straightforward and accessible novel. The narrative describes a lover's revenge tragedy and self-consciously foregrounds its debt to *Othello* through parallels, allusions, and a small number of explicit references. Through eleven chapters, Barnes plots the descent of Graham Hendrick's sanity from the exuberance of his

first encounters with Ann Mears to the self-slaughter that closes the
book. It is most easily seen as a study of obsession and compulsion
shot through with humour and pathos but some recognition of its
historical moment is important to an understanding of the novel's
standpoint.

At the narrative's start, Graham meets Ann at Jack's flat at Repton
Gardens in April 1977. This is the same flat in which he will, in the
novel's final chapter, murder Jack, tie up Ann, now his wife, and then
commit suicide. This final chapter is entitled 'The horse and the
crocodile', a reference to the book's first epigraph:

> Man finds himself in the predicament that nature has endowed him
> essentially with three brains which, despite great differences in structure,
> must function together and communicate with one another. The oldest
> of these brains is basically reptilian. The second has been inherited from
> the lower mammals, and the third is a late mammalian development,
> which . . . has made man peculiarly man. Speaking allegorically of these
> brains within a brain, we might imagine that when the psychiatrist bids
> the patient to lie on the couch, he is asking him to stretch out along-
> side a horse and a crocodile. (Paul D. MacLean, *Journal of Nervous and
> Mental Diseases*, vol. CXXXV, no. 4, October 1962)

According to MacLean's theory, which equates animals with lower
or more primitive sides to human nature, each person has not one
but three brains: neomammalian (the human – residing in the brain
cortex), paleomammalian (the horse – forebrain) and reptilian (the
crocodile – back and mid brain). The reptilian crocodile might bring
to mind Jack's behaviour, in which the satisfaction of his basic physical desires and their associated pleasurable activities (indiscriminate
sex, flatulence, drinking, smoking) is uninhibited by higher interpersonal concerns involving other people's well-being or sensibilities.
The paleomammalian horse brain, which is associated with sexual
arousal, memory, and addiction, might suggest Graham's jealousy and
suspicion, which have licensed the killings of the book's final chapter. This would associate Ann with the more evolved neomammalian
brain that distinguishes humans. Yet, almost the entire novel has been
striated with these co-selves, in MacLean's taxonomy, stretched out
alongside the patient.

Each chapter title possibly also alludes to some aspect of the story's
concern with MacLean's animal parallels. 'Three suits and a violin',
the opening chapter, references what Aldous Huxley took from his
burning home, rather than his manuscripts, for example. It suggests

a set of priorities that are unfathomable to most other people but point toward the spartan choices of portable property Graham makes when he leaves his first wife Barbara. Presaging and then paralleling Graham's emotional rawness, Barbara remains throughout the book a bitter, revenge-driven character, whose satisfaction at Graham's failure is easier to imagine than her compassion over the death of her daughter's father (cf. the closing line of Chapter One: 'he would say to himself, now that I've got Ann, at least now I'll be properly mourned', BS, p. 25). However, according to Graham, Barbara has a peculiar perspective on her feelings, which are made to work hard for her: 'Barbara's sense of betrayal wasn't as sharp as she let him continue to believe. She had always been a Marxist about emotions, believing that they shouldn't just exist for themselves, but should do some work if they were to eat' (BS, p. 31). To an extent this sardonic example of English pragmatism and martial bitterness indicates that the book is firmly in the comic mode despite its subject matter resting on the twin impulses towards life and death, eros and thanatos.

In contrast to Barbara, Graham seems more and more to be made to work for his emotions. 'In flagrante' alludes to his first cinematic encounters with Ann's 'adulteries' – on-screen dalliances with other men that preceded their marriage. Graham at this early stage in his fascination with Ann's previous career can take an objective, critically detached approach to 'betrayal' when watching her on film: 'It was always bad art that one examined to get the clearest idea of the form's basic conventions' (BS, p. 27). His professional academic mindset positions him as someone interested in questions of genre and not human emotion.

Prompted to see a first film featuring Ann only by a deception of Barbara's, Graham, who has eschewed cinemagoing for many years, repeatedly seeks out opportunities effectively to spy on Ann's past. His trips to the cinema have a primary purpose of discovering Ann on screen in bedroom scenes with other men. However, as the narrative unfolds, Graham is increasingly unable to separate fact from fiction, or past from present. As a historian, the past lives strongly for him, and researching what happened 'before' is his life's work. In the first film he sees, *Over the Moon*, Ann plays a 'viciously peroxided' (BS, p. 28) woman who is only seen on camera in bed. Graham is amused by this first encounter with Ann's screen personae but his daughter by Barbara, Alice, thinks Ann's 'a tart' and a 'rubbish' actress. Ironically, given what follows, Graham replies that Ann is only 'acting' (BS, p. 30) but Alice asserts 'I just think she did it too darn well', which sits oddly with her opinion that Ann is a poor actress but establishes the sense of equivalence between Ann's on- and off-screen identities that will dominate Graham's thoughts for the rest of the book. This also sounds one of the keynotes of Barnes's books: the vicissitudes of imagination. The advantages but also dangers of a vivid imagination in *Metroland* lie partly at the root of Chris and Toni's observational exercises in the National Gallery in London: they are both susceptible to quasi-logical flights of speculation but unable to gain a perspective on the correspondences they expect to find between art and aesthetic response. This is an element in Barnes's work that will appear repeatedly through to *Arthur & George*, two figures marked by an overactive and an underactive imagination that under-lines divergent views of truth and reality.

The figure in *Before She Met Me* who understands the power of the imagination, but controls it for the purposes of writing fiction, is Graham's friend Jack. Jack's view is that all marriages have their burdens and Graham's is to come to terms with his feelings about Ann's past. Graham wishes to resolve this intellectually using his skills as an academic, but Jack advises him to seek lower-level 'reptilian' solutions such as masturbation or adultery. Jack adds that he is happy to welcome Graham any time on to his 'psychocouch' but Graham, already hooked on investigating Ann's celluloid past, merely wonders if he can catch a further film, *The Good Time*, and see another of Ann's 'adulteries'.[2] Jack concludes that Graham 'loves Ann too much' and that his fascination with her ex-lovers is an unhealthy extension of his psychological and sexual insecurity. This is underlined by revelations of Graham's obsession with Ann, which encompasses an emotional attachment to the toilet paper Ann has used, which suggest both Graham's fetishism and his vulnerability.

When the couple attempt to take a holiday to relax and enjoy each other, Graham's jealousy merely spreads abroad. Reminding the reader of one of *Metroland*'s signature phrases, 'sex is travel', Graham has to cross Italian destinations off their holiday list because Ann has visited them before with other men. Here as elsewhere, Graham is conflicted: 'I can't explain it. I certainly can't justify it. I'm glad you went to Italy . . . I know it all in steps, I know the logic. All of it makes me glad. It just makes me want to cry as well' (BS, p. 55). Graham also examines Ann's books to try to find which have been given to her; the first is the grotesque fantasy by Mervyn Peake, *Gormenghast*, which hints at the modern gothic absurdity of *Before She Met Me*, but the second is Graham Greene's *The End of the Affair*. This signals on Barnes's part a parallel between *Before She Met Me* and Greene's story of Maurice Bendrix's deep suspicions about his lover's relationship with a rival, who he thinks is another man but who proves to be in a sense both real and imaginary – God. The closeness between the names Bendrix and Hendrick also suggests an indebtedness.

To agree that they should expunge their own illicit affair from the historical record, Ann goes to see Jack. As Jack is a novelist, his business, like that of Ann's film career, is rooted in fiction and he seems uncomfortable with the unadorned truth, preferring to spin his own version of events on most subjects, including his adulteries. By contrast, Graham is a historian with a desire to fathom truths. However, his biggest problem is with his imagination, which has little feel for the ontological difference of the fictional worlds professionally inhabited by Ann and Jack. Reminding the reader again of the epigraph from MacLean, Jack explains to Graham that the human brain is 'One layer of Four-Eyes, two layers of Sawn-Offs', with the second underdeveloped layers being 'the ones that control our emotions, make us kill people, fuck other people's wives, vote Tory, kick the dog' (BS, p. 74). Jack is an observer of others professionally and habitually. Consequently, despite his cynicism, he understands human beings much better than Graham does, but Jack's knowledge is used to satisfy his own desires. Like Barbara, he makes his emotions work for him. By contrast, Graham's dreams become lurid and self-lacerating when his unconscious concocts vivid sexual situations between Ann and her co-stars. This illustrates Graham's predicament as outlined by Jack: 'Most people have got the Sawn-Offs well under their thumb, I'd say. Most people control their emotions, don't they? It may not be easy, but they do. I mean, they control them *enough*' (BS, p. 76).

Having ruled out numerous possibilities because of Graham's jealousy over Ann's geographical virginity, the couple embark on a holiday to France. A central scene occurs at Clermont l'Hérault at a time when Ann is reading Daphne du Maurier's *Rebecca* – another parallel text of remarriage, an unresolved past, and jealousy – and Graham is reading a history book about the locality. He learns several unusual details about the area, including the fact that the local priests used to have sex on dunghills. On discovering this, he proceeds to read the most unpleasant passages to Ann. Again, the conjoining of one of the more cerebral aspects of human culture, religious aspiration, with the most animalistic, literal sex in the dirt, results in ill-feeling between the couple and this leads on to a scene in which they make violent love despite Ann's period, underlining the point that Graham's attempts to rationalise his possessive feelings about Ann are in every sense partial. Barnes may be alluding here to the theme of 'the beast and the monk', perhaps most famously discussed in English literature in Chapter 22 of E. M. Forster's *Howards End*: 'Only connect the prose and the passion, and both will be exalted, and human love will be seen at its height. Live in fragments no longer. Only connect, and the beast and the monk, robbed of the isolation that is life to either, will die.' Forster says that without the Nietzschean 'rainbow bridge' that brings together the prose and the passion of life 'we are meaningless fragments, half monks, half beasts, unconnected arches that have never joined into a man'.[3] In the psychological bestiary of *Before She Met Me*, the beast is the horse, which represents the passion and sense that Graham cannot simultaneously master. Its literary symbolism might be suggested by D. H. Lawrence's deployment of the horse in his fiction, such as Gerald Crich's aggressive disciplining of his red mare in Chapter 9 of *Women in Love*, but is better explained in his non-fiction writings.[4] For example, Lawrence writes in his posthumously published meditation on the Book of Revelation, *Apocalypse*:

> How the horse dominated the mind of the early races, especially of the Mediterranean! . . . And as a symbol he roams the dark underworld meadows of the soul. . . . Within the last fifty years man has lost the horse. Now man is lost. Man is lost to life and power – an underling and a wastrel. While horses thrashed the streets of London, London lived.[5]

Jung thought the horse represented intuition but that it could also be a symbol of the human body. Influenced by Jung, Lawrence concluded that the horse symbolised a destructive sensuality which could overwhelm the individual, combining terror and beauty. He writes in 'Fantasia of the Unconscious':

> For example, a man has a persistent passionate fear-dream about horses. He suddenly finds himself among great, physical horses, which may suddenly go wild . . . The automatic pseudo-soul, which has got the sensual nature repressed, would like to keep it repressed. Whereas the greatest desire of the living spontaneous soul is that this very male sensual nature, represented as a menace, shall be actually accomplished in life.[6]

Also drawing on literary roots from the same period, one of Barnes's chapter titles, 'The Feminian sandstones', takes its title from a poem by Rudyard Kipling: 'The gods of the copybook headings'. The poem was written shortly after the Great War (1919) and advocates a pragmatic stoicism centred on a belief that the only sure things are the truths of nature and the certainty that humanity will go on repeating itself: 'As it will be in the future, it was at the birth of Man'. The Femian interglacial period occurred 140,000–120,000 years ago and the poem suggests that little has changed in human psychology since. Jack quotes the first two lines of this verse to Graham, but the second couplet is additionally relevant to the novel's ending:

> On the first Feminian Sandstones we were promised the Fuller Life
> (Which started by loving our neighbour and ended by loving his wife)
> Till our women had no more children and the men lost reason and faith,
> And the Gods of the Copybook Headings said: 'The Wages of Sin is Death.'

By this stage, Ann is already watching Graham as if he were a potential suicide, while Graham ponders three questions, which would be answered by Kipling's Gods who seem to keep in their copybooks the moral debit and credit records of humanity: Why does human jealousy exist in relation to love? Why can jealousy apply retrospectively? And why is jealousy still flourishing in the last quarter of the twentieth century? The novel suggests that these are the unchanged provinces of the horse and the crocodile – whose sway over the emotions it is not easy for the rational part for the brain to control according to Jack.

Graham spends a day with his daughter Alice and broods on the causes of his jealousy, finding a parallel with his students' occasional disappointment in history, or at least in historians, because good has not, as they see it, triumphed over evil. The past should have been otherwise and a 'retrospective sense of justice' is in operation, Graham conjectures, making a comparison with his retrospective jealousy (BS, pp. 114–15). Graham sees no practical benefit to ill-feeling about a past that did not involve you while Jack argues that it is a quirk of marriage, or at least monogamy, to be jealous. Graham wonders if it is in fact something to do with the phenomenon of romantic love necessarily involving failure, yet it is only later that a more pertinent question arises for him: 'You thought about your brain, when you did, as something you used – put things into and got out

answers. Now, suddenly, you felt as if it were using you . . . what
if your brain became your enemy?' (BS, p. 132). This is at the heart
of the comedy and pathos of *Before She Met Me*, in which divisions
within the mind are the source of self-harm. Jack lives happily with
his contradictions, but also places his own satisfaction and equanimity
above that of others, while Graham tries to combine irreconcilable
drives to rationalism and idealism in ways that prohibit him from
mental integration or balance, leading to deeply dysfunctional
behaviours.

Barnes references Freud's putative observation that 'Sometimes
a cigar is only a cigar', implying that not everything is symbolic of
something else, nor are interpretations equally valid. It is probably
delusional to see the world as always metaphorical or actions as always
containing a hidden meaning, which is the conclusion Christopher
reaches in *Metroland*. Graham however has moved from a comparatively healthy intellectual interest in correspondences to a hermeneutic
paranoia: a disabling level of distrust about the meaning of everything.
'Sometimes a cigar . . .' focuses on a party that Ann suggests and which
prompts Graham's suspicions about Jack and Ann when he sees a
kiss and a caress. Ann suggests these actions mean nothing – a cigar
is sometimes just a cigar – but Graham sees them as proof not only
that Ann and Jack have had an affair in the past but that they are
still having one. Graham decides also to concoct a plan to prove this,
involving Jack's wife Sue. He arranges a lunch in London with her
and casually lets on that he knows about an ongoing affair between
Jack and Ann. Not wanting to seem ignorant, Sue plays along that
she already knows, falsely confirming Graham's suspicions. She also
explains about Jack's indulgence in 'The Stanley Spencer syndrome':
that artists need to have experience, particularly sexual, and this is
simply in their nature. What is more pertinently in human nature
according to the novel returns us to the title of the final chapter: 'The
horse and the crocodile'.

There is a matter-of-factness about this denouement, which
describes the story's brutal ending without heightening the language
or striving for emotional impact. One implication is that in Graham's
mind his actions are logical; another is that the novel has established
the plausibly of an ending such as this. Graham wants above all
for his final actions not to seem like a film, and the avoidance of
cliché in the denouement is also apparent in the eschewal of conventional fictional tropes. The book is light on science and aims not to

provide any stance on evolutionary psychology, but wants to explore the effects of excessive jealousy and the often troubled relationship between emotional drives and ratiocination. The ending is not likely, any more than the ending of *Othello* is likely, but is in some ways best seen as a metaphor for the emotional destruction wrought by intense jealousy on the lover, on the loved one, and the putative other lover, making literal the desires that drive Graham's psyche to obliterate and to tie down.

In some ways, the book's final scene is prefigured in many small earlier textual aspects from the opening pages onwards. There are the many references to cutting up meat or offal, foreshadowing the butchery at the novel's end (e.g. when he sees Jack and talks about finishing Ann's meat from her plate). There is also the sense of untapped wells of emotion released by Ann in Graham:

> Ann had introduced him not just to Pleasure . . . but to its intricate approaches . . . Grateful as he was to her for teaching him, . . . he sometimes ran up against a residual, nervous vexation that Ann had got there before him. After all, he was seven years older than her. In bed, for instance, her confident easiness often seemed to him to be show-ing up (criticising, mocking almost) his own cautious, stiff-jointed awkwardness (BS, p. 14).

Graham is in many ways ill-equipped to deal with the feelings Ann provokes in him: 'For at least ten years he had found a diminishing use for his body', seeing himself as 'merely a brain lodged in a con-tainer' (BS, p. 12). Graham's absence of identity makes him more vulnerable to any threat to his happiness with Ann: 'Whenever Ann was away on business he missed her not sexually, but morally'; 'He envied the things she touched'; 'He felt frustrated at not being allowed to be her, not even for a day' (BS, pp. 24–5). Graham emerges as an innocent who cannot cope with experience in his own life and in his wife's history. His first wife Barbara speaks in Chapter 5 of how he is like a 'schoolboy' and this echoes with the broader presentation of him as someone unable to comprehend or cope with the darker qualities of the adult world.

There are many elements to the book that can be related to Barnes's overall output in terms of the interest in love, jealousy, and the *ménage à trois*, but the book is also about reading the world. Graham's professional role as an interpreter of texts is entirely inadequate when it comes to looking at life, and even his interest in biography is reduced to a search for sex (BS, p. 126). His suspicions concerning Jack and Ann are fuelled by a textual analysis of his friend's fiction. He reads and rereads Jack's novels for clues that will reveal the ways in which Jack wrote references to Ann into his narratives. Graham's conclusions are worrying for an historical interpreter whose job involves reconstructing the past from textual evidence: 'There could be no doubt at all. Jack's affair with Ann had started in 1971, had continued during the time he was first getting to know Ann, and then through all their marriage' (BS, p. 154).

Merritt Moseley proposes that Graham follows an opposite path to Christopher Lloyd, moving from the ordinary to the extraordinary,[7] but it is also true that they have characteristics in common. Both are drawn to the textual and the sensual but both are unwilling or unable to embrace the wilder sides of life. Beside Toni and Jack, and indeed beside Marion and Ann, they seem contained and repressed, but the one is contented, the other conflicted. Graham's descent charts the course that Christopher might have followed when he discovered Marion had been unfaithful.

Narrated in the third person, *Before She Met Me* would probably be more accurately but less engagingly entitled 'Before She Met Him'. The novel may accordingly be understood as a black humoured variation on the medieval French tradition of the fabliau: a short comic verse tale, whose preferred theme was the cuckolded dupe, of non-aristocratic characters delighting in the obscene. Most famous in England in examples such as Chaucer's *Miller's Tale*, the many variants of the fabliau in English farce feed into the modern postwar comic realist novel that is in the lineage that leads on to a post-1960s version in Barnes's fable of the human, the horse, and the crocodile. Or the historian, the writer, and the actress.

Before She Met Me is a well-crafted satirical short novel with a clear dramatic structure, setting and power. Its use of imagery and metaphor is heavy-handed and this is something that Barnes has honed over the course of his career, with subtler and richer similes and analogies evident in the later fiction. The dark humour is also heavier in this novel than elsewhere, and *Before She Met Me* is the foremost of Barnes's novel to align itself with the *Duffy* stories that he was writing as Dan Kavanagh at the same time. His next novel would take him in a very different direction and bring to the fore the invention, wit, and experimentation that have become Barnes's hallmarks.

Notes

1 This epigraph is from Molière's play *Les Fourberies de Scapin* (*Scapin's Deceits*, 1667): 'Il vaut mieux encore d'être marié que mort.' Scapin, Act 1, Scene 4: 'It's better to be married than to be dead.'
2 After learning that Ann slept with her co-star on one job he decides to see the film again, and again.
3 E. M. Forster, *Howards End*, Penguin: Harmondsworth, 1985, p. 187.
4 The colour is significant: 'The red horse is choler: not mere anger, but natural fieryness, what we call passion.' D. H. Lawrence, *Apocalypse*, Penguin: Harmondsworth, 1974, p. 62.
5 Ibid., pp. 60–1.
6 D. H. Lawrence, 'Fantasia of the unconscious' in *Fantasia of the Unconscious/Psychoanalysis of the Unconscious*, Penguin: Harmondsworth, 1971, pp. 170–1.
7 Merritt Moseley, *Understanding Julian Barnes*, Columbia, South Carolina: University of South Carolina Press, 1997, p. 54.

3

What happened to the truth is not recorded: *Flaubert's Parrot*

> I thought of Flaubert's Parrot when I started writing it as obviously an unofficial and informal, unconventional sort of novel – an upside down novel, a novel in which there was an infrastructure of fiction and very strong elements of non-fiction, sometimes whole chapters which were nothing but arranged facts.[1]

After two comparatively conventional novels anatomising modern love, Barnes's next book contains by contrast an unusual range of narrative types, including apocrypha, autobiography, bestiary, biography, chronology, criticism, dialogue, dictionary, essay, exam, guide, and manifesto. *Flaubert's Parrot* is a novel at one remove: partly a novel about a novelist, partly a novel about a man obsessed with a novelist, and partly a novel about the business of novel-writing. It is also a strange kind of life-writing about the real Gustave Flaubert, a portrait of whose life becomes ever more complex as the identification of his parrot becomes more complicated, and the fictional Geoffrey Braithwaite, whose life-story slowly emerges in glimpses, but in a way that leaves the reader with questions, as Braithwaite has of Flaubert. This is one way in which Barnes challenges the homogeneous formal approach of conventional biography, when in fact 'Nature is always a mixture of genres'. (FP, p. 134) Barnes's many prose genres taken together question definitions of fact and fiction, history and story, truth and opinion, and the method of his third novel stands in stark contrast to its narrator Geoffrey Braithwaite's quest to find the 'real' Flaubert's parrot: a search that broadens out from one candidate to a whole roomful. Finding the parrot is also akin to a difficult task that, in Alison Lee's words, is 'tantamount to finding the author's true voice', which cannot 'be located that easily' (FP, p. 22).[2] With nods to the realist novel's attempt to render life through the accumulation of detail and the modernist novel's similar preoccupation with the artist's interior life, the question of verisimilitude in fiction is implicitly interrogated in the novel, as art has a different relationship with social and personal reality from history's, drawing on emotional veracities that underpin all of Barnes's work but which often confound the language of rational analysis.

In critical reviews, Barnes's work has often raised questions of genre and the boundaries of the novel, but these issues have quietened over the years as the boundaries have been challenged more often. *Flaubert's Parrot* is striated with fictional invention but also has essayistic sections of a kind that more commonly appear in magazines and periodicals. Yet the only form that seems capacious enough to accommodate the variety of genres that Barnes employs is the novel. Randall Jarrell's oft-quoted playful description of a novel as 'A prose narrative of some length that has something wrong with it' appears to suit *Flaubert's Parrot* better than most; indeed the definition seems to work better for novels by Barnes than by Dickens or George Eliot. Barnes himself said of the novel in a letter to his publisher's editor: 'So it's a book a) about Flaubert; b) about writing (not 19thc writing: writing now as well); and c) a semi-fiction in itself.'[3] It is this mix-ture that led to some critics arguing simply that Barnes breaks the novel's boundaries. More useful might be the observation that his approach to writing, emphasising formal experimentation and a reflective treatment of art, sits more comfortably, like the Irish strain through Swift and Sterne to Beckett and O'Brien, in a European tradi-tion of writing from *Don Quixote* and *Gargantua and Pantagruel* to Milan Kundera's *The Book of Laughter and Forgetting* and Italo Calvino's *If on a Winter's Night a Traveller*. In this tradition, Flaubert himself stands not as the apotheosis of realist technique but as a scrupulous experimenter who took the novel in new directions. Having used Flaubert's *L'Éducation Sentimentale* as a touchstone for his first novel, Barnes employs more of Flaubert's writings to com-plement *Flaubert's Parrot*, from the story of his cuckolded doctor Geoffrey Braithwaite echoing the plot of *Madame Bovary* to his use of *Trois Contes*:[4] 'Three stories contend within me. One about Flaubert, one about Ellen [Ellen Braithwaite shares not just initials with Emma Bovary], one about myself. My own is the simplest of the three' (FP, pp. 85–6)[5]. For Barnes as for Flaubert, there are no simple stories, and, if there is one message that *Flaubert's Parrot* wears on its sleeve, it is this rejection of simplicity, underlined repeatedly in the novel from its start, with the description of a game, to its end, with Geoffrey Braithwaite left staring at three stuffed parrots.

The chase for the bird of the title can be understood in many ways. In one sense it is a search for a specific dead parrot: the one Flaubert owned at the time of writing 'Un coeur simple' from *Three Tales*, and which would have served as a model for the parrot, Loulou, mistaken for the holy spirit in the story.[6] At this level Barnes's novel can be understood as a straightforward tale: a quest narrative. Braithwaite soon finds however that there are two birds that seem to fit the bill: each has claims pressed for it, and from this the difficulties of establishing the 'real' bird, and what that means, proliferate.

The book spends some time on the parrot itself but it would be as helpful to see the title as metaphoric and connotative as it would be to see it as denotative. The title can also certainly be seen as metonymic, referring to the quest for an author's identity through biographical research, rather than through reading the works. Braithwaite's search for Flaubert's parrot is an attempt to get to know the author, and the bird hunt is in part shorthand for that investigation.[7] But, by the end of the book there are not two but scores of parrots, and the search for the correct bird, like the authentic Flaubert, has flown off in multiple directions, mocking the attempt to find the person behind the writings as a flight of fancy that is largely folly. The best result is a net to throw over and constrict the author, whose life stares through the holes in the story, and the worst is a tissue of lies: 'What chance would the craftiest biographer stand against the subject who saw him coming and decided to amuse himself?' (FP, p. 38) For Barnes, the only truth of any significance lies in the writings and the author is best left anonymous despite the reader's temptation to indulge in literary 'train-spotting'. A parrot imitates speech, adding nothing to the learned words but their repetition; the bird may be amusing or annoying, but it is unlikely to say something new. Critics have been tempted to suggest that either Braithwaite or even Barnes is the 'real' Flaubert's parrot, but these seem harsh assessments and to miss both of the final points that there is no resolution to the question and even if there were, it would be a mere brute fact that simply satisfied curiosity.

The many parrots are from one angle analogous to the many stories told in the book; most of them are about Flaubert but none of them is particularly revealing about Flaubert's writing (the closest we get to this is in passages such as the discussion of the colour of Emma

Bovary's eyes). Most of the other strands to the narrative are about Braithwaite. Barnes has said:

> [Braithwaite's] presence is intended to do two things: 1) Allow more points of access, and a greater range of response, to Flaubert: the narrator, being basically quite sane but given to bursts of extremity, can go out on a limb for Flaubert, hypothesize wildly, put contradictory points of view, etc, which are impossible with a traditional lit-crit approach. 2) Tie the stories together. The narrator's presence runs through the book, sometimes faintly, sometimes pushily; as we read, the subplot of his life develops, until, in the final story, there is a tying-off of his personal history. Also, having the narrator as a character in the book, he can usefully have his life bounced off that of Flaubert, and vice versa.[8]

Barnes has said that the chapters were not written in order and their arrangement need not have been exactly as it is, though they have been sequenced. The book conceals its artifice but also documents the essentially escapist nature of art. Like a parrot it ceaselessly repeats itself as questions are put once and then twice and then again, while Flaubertian *bons mots* are deployed and then reiterated, as when the three preconditions for happiness 'stupidity, selfishness and good health' are noted with regard to Flaubert (FP, p. 147) and then revisited in the life of Braithwaite and his wife (FP, pp. 166–7).

A celebration of literature and love as well as a reflection on loss and grief, *Flaubert's Parrot* is a threnody to fidelity and a hymn to infidelity. It seeks to find something positive in uncertainties while arguing that the past is unrecoverable, the truth is ungraspable, and attempts to capture the writer are full of holes. In this, while deprecating Sartre for his views on Flaubert, the book is as much existential as postmodernist: Braithwaite escapes his own life into the writer's because he is compelled to fill his time and (re)direct his thoughts. As with all Barnes's writings, any attempt to find meaning in *Flaubert's Parrot* is conducted with an ironic sense that it will reside somewhere between fabulation and projection. Death is inevitable and God the greatest fiction, (even) though truth can be found in the beauty and consolation of art. This is not the radical scepticism of postmodernism but the frustration of modernism: Barnes does not seem to deny the existence of reality, but he does appear repeatedly to question our ability to know it. Instead, we can seek to be more or less deceived about our lives (Geoffrey Braithwaite), the lives of those closest to us (Ellen Braithwaite), and those lives we seek (Gustave Flaubert) if we 'chase the writer' (FP, p. 12).

Chapter Four of *Flaubert's Parrot* closes with a series of dog stories, the first three of which end with a statement about how what happened to the dog was not recorded. The fourth ends with a disputed dog story, of which there are two versions, ending with the statement 'What happened to the truth is not recorded' (FP, p. 65). This last shaggy dog story concerns imitation: in one version a dragoman is able to trade barks with a distant dog, allowing travellers to find their way to shelter; in the other, more prosaic account – Flaubert's – it was a policeman's pistol that entered into dialogue with the barking dog. Is the first version enlivened by embellishment or is the second misrecorded? Similarly, elsewhere in *Flaubert's Parrot* there are choices between competing truths: between rival parrots, for example, and between interpretations of Ellen Braithwaite's death. Unlike the deluded Graham Hendrick in *Before She Met Me*, Geoffrey Braithwaite appears to be troubled by his wife's actual infidelities: 'Should a husband punish her, or forgive her? . . . At first I was hurt; at first I minded, I thought less of myself' (FP, p. 162). Like Graham Hendrick, Braithwaite is interested in the past; he is not an historian but he is exercised by the receding coast of time fading from view and memory.

The chapter called 'Snap!' is about coincidences, or when two things match, as though a literary hand is at work organising life like art (cf. the discussion of Baudelairian 'correpondences' in *Metroland*). The game of snap proceeds by two people in turns laying down a card from their stash. If the face value of two consecutive cards is the same then the first person to say 'Snap' wins all the exposed cards. The game is totally random, assuming a good shuffle of the deck beforehand. The coming together of two cards with identical values is therefore both highly predictable as a phenomenon and almost impossible to predict accurately. However, Braithwaite does not care for this planned view of a created world with a grand purpose. Instead he likes to think life is 'chaotic, . . . permanently . . . crazy' and that the only 'certainty' is 'human ignorance, brutality and folly' (FP, p. 66). Without commenting on the fact, Braithwaite then creates a seeming correspondence by beginning the chapter berating a middle-class bourgeois habit of opining how life imitates art – 'It's just like Anthony Powell' – and then telling an anecdote in which he attended a dinner party at which 'the seven other people present had all just finished reading *A Dance to the Music of Time*', Powell's series of novels. Braithwaite finds something 'cheap and sentimental' about coincidences in books, and so this double use of Powell might be called ironical in the context, wryly illustrating its own point. Except Braithwaite then implies he distrusts ironies as merely 'smart' coincidences (FP, p. 67) beloved of writers like Flaubert (and Barnes). He asks if 'ironies accrete around the ironist?' and then proceeds to adumbrate some Flaubertian examples, concluding with an aside that, 'if you don't like these ironies, I have others' (68). The chapter concludes with three more extended examples and a final reflection on whether the apprehension of seeming correspondences (*déjà vu*, synchronicity, etc.) 'read as brute coincidence, silky irony, or brave, far-sighted modernism', or might 'just have been a joke on us?' (FP, p. 73) In other words, perhaps Flaubert saw us 'coming and decided to amuse himself?' (FP, p. 38) and this is 'the irony about the irony' (FP, p. 69) when we see the nuanced but apposite Flaubertian observation: 'the sort of exchange, in which the everyday tampers with the sublime, that we like to think of proprietorially as typical of our own wry and unfoolable age' (FP, p. 69).

Much the same might be said about the artful way in which Barnes has plotted correspondences between the life and writings of Flaubert and the story of Geoffrey Braithwaite, and there is a temptation to think that the joke is simply on the reader. Yet, this is a response only to the ludic element in Barnes's writing, which sits, uncomfortably for some, alongside his novels' more engaged and emotional undercurrent. Which is to say that Braithwaite's interest in not being anyone's fool – the bourgeois Powellians, the ironist, the knowing author – needs to be read as part of the fiction, linked to a painful life story that hinges on deception and duplicity: on adultery and suicide, or killing (FP, p. 97). The narrator is a man wounded by his misreading of his own life's events and deeply concerned that the joke is on him: 'My wife . . . died. My children are scattered now; they write whenever guilt impels. They have their own lives, naturally. "Life! Life! To have erections!" I was reading that Flaubertian exclamation the other day. It made me feel like a stone statue with a patched upper thigh' (FP, p. 13). The novel's epigraph also has a resonance here as Braithwaite (or/and Barnes) quotes Flaubert on writing a friend's biography: 'you must do it as if you were taking *revenge* for him' (letter to Ernest Feydeau, 1872).

Concern with mimesis spans literary history, and *Flaubert's Parrot* encompasses the perspectives of classical philosophy and art theory as well as the social engagement of realism, modernism's desire to break with the past, and many tropes of postmodernism in fiction. Examples from the novel can be cited to support almost any view on its categorisation, but it has most commonly been grouped with a crop of meta-historical novels from the 1980s that comment self-consciously on (the relation they have to) historical or biographical material and 'have in common an intent not just to delight readers with fascinating characters and compelling stories from earlier eras but also to stimulate an interest in the methods by which we know the past and the uses to which we put that knowledge'.[9] The characteristics of such literary postmodernist approaches to history can be outlined briefly: an underlining of the shared discursive, constructed and narrative aspects of fiction and historiography; a deliberate mix of imaginary and historical material to subvert the certainties of historical knowledge, as opposed to 'fabulation'; a questioning of whether the past can be known; a belief that since there is no 'value-neutral' historical discourse there is also no basis for positivist concepts like objectivity and transparency of representation; an awareness of the provisional nature of historical knowledge; a belief that truth is not obtainable but can be a Platonic ideal to warn against relativity and passivity; the explicit recognition of connections between official historical versions and political power; a rejection of theories of historical patterning for a sense of entropy reflecting history's discontinuity and supercomplexity.

In keeping with this, *Flaubert's Parrot* ponders whether the writer is 'much more than a sophisticated parrot' (FP, p. 18), because language, as Roland Barthes argued, speaks us (Barthes is mentioned on p. 84). But, in modernist style, Barnes also draws attention to Flaubert's felicity with words while quoting his contention from *Madame Bovary* that 'Language is like a cracked kettle on which we beat out tunes for bears to dance to, while all the time we long to move the stars to pity' (FP, p. 19). Such dichotomies, or dualisms, pervade the novel, from the 'duplicate parrots' (FP, p. 22) that may be Flaubert's to the French writer's own ambivalence on most subjects from life ('like soup with lots of hairs floating on the surface', FP, p. 34) to work ('I love my work with a frantic and perverted love, as an ascetic loves the hair-shirt which scratches his belly', FP, p. 34). These comments appear in the third of Braithwaite's three Flaubert chronologies, each notable for its own characteristics. The first emphasises success; the second failure and misery; the third an awareness of life's duality: 'I have always tried to live in an ivory tower, but a tide of shit is beating at its walls, threatening to undermine it' (FP, p. 36). Throughout the book are reflections that ask whether they mark 'success or failure? Remembrance or self-indulgence?' (FP, p. 161)

Braithwaite asks this question about the loss of a loved one – where memory may be both a pleasure and a pain. Flaubert also articulates the frustrations of a life in which writing serves a function as task and consolation: 'I still carry on turning out my sentences, like a bourgeois turning out napkin rings on a lathe in his attic. It gives me something to do, and it affords me some private pleasure' (FP, p. 36). Barnes has noted that he thinks *Before She Met Me* is his funniest book, when to many readers it seems his most sardonic and horrific. Similarly, while many reviewers praised *Flaubert's Parrot* as both funny and delightful, it is at best ambivalent, at worst sad and mournful. 'Is it splendid, or stupid', Braithwaite asks by quoting Flaubert, 'to take life seriously?'

Flaubert's remark on language as a cracked kettle is repeated by Braithwaite in his own most revelatory chapter, 'Pure story'. This is a companion piece to the many other meditations on love and death that course through Barnes's work, including the uxorious half chapter of *A History of the World* and the ruminations of *Nothing to Be Frightened of*. Braithwaite recounts his own life with the sense of narrative possibilities he observed in accounts of Flaubert's life, and this is undertaken with pathos and resignation: 'You talk, and you find the language of bereavement foolishly inadequate . . . I loved her; we were happy; I miss her. She didn't love me; we were unhappy; I miss her' (FP, p. 161). Both language and narrative are unable to convey the emotional complexity of life. Braithwaite begins to tell an anecdote, a story, that will convey something of his wife. He draws on Flaubert's words, and on the techniques of biography, but then decides 'I'll start again', only to begin the following paragraph with the same phrase, 'I'll start again' (FP, p. 162). This is, as the chapter and Braithwaite are keen to tell us: 'Pure story'. In Barnes's writings this means many things, including the suggestion that the only pure story is the utterly fictitious one; yet that is not Braithwaite's meaning: 'I have to hypothesise a little. I have to fictionalise (though that's not what I meant when I called this a pure story)' (FP, p. 165). For Braithwaite he means by 'pure story' that it is only through plausible, testable supposition – hypothesis and experimentation – that he can conjecture his way towards an understanding of his wife's life. He says that he has 'to invent' his 'way to the truth' (FP, 165) in order to understand her passions, which contrast with his own: 'she didn't have some rash devotion to a dead foreigner to sustain her' (FP, p. 166). This moves us closer to a third meaning of the chapter title and an important aspect of Barnes's convictions because 'Pure story' in his work also means that truth resides in artifice (and not, for example, in the discourses that claim to deliver it, such as religion or politics).

But, finally, Ellen Braithwaite's is a 'true story' (FP, p. 86) of life lived, like Tess Durbeyfield's, or Emma Bovary's, where at her death she 'wasn't corrupted. Hers is a pure story' (FP, p. 168). For Braithwaite, Ellen lived her life and 'believed the best' while her husband indulged in 'love's favourite perversion' in 'wanting to know the worst' (FP, p. 126), and turned to books for his purity: 'perhaps love for a writer is the purest, the steadiest form of love' (FP, p. 127). For others, books are the thing and they 'prefer reading' (FP, p. 171). Braithwaite knows Flaubert better than Ellen, but only knows him through words: 'Books are where things are explained to you; life is where things aren't. I'm not surprised some people prefer books. Books make sense of life. The only problem is that the lives they make sense of are other people's lives, never your own' (FP, p. 168). In other words, art orders, as E. M. Forster argued: 'Works of art, in my opinion, are the only objects in the material universe to possess internal order, and that is why, though I don't believe that only art matters, I do believe in Art for Art's sake.'[10]

Flaubert's Parrot begins with a tale of a statue of Flaubert; but the statue with which the novel begins is soon qualified: 'This statue isn't the original one' (FP, p. 11). Instead there are several monuments to the honoured dead, replicas of an original; multiplied likenesses. The first statue was taken away by the Germans in the war and a 'new image' created. Or rather three were made, one in metal and two in stone. The stone ones have decayed but the copper and tin statue has not: 'Perhaps the foundry's assurances can be believed: perhaps this second-impression statue will last. But I see no particular grounds for confidence. Nothing much else to do with Flaubert has ever lasted' (FP, p. 12). Imitations abound and their fidelity is always questionable: likenesses taken from likenesses that are not thought will last, copies that will fade or be lost. A book concerned throughout with imitation, *Flaubert's Parrot* begins where *Metroland* ends: with a question mark over theories of correspondence. Also, the correspondences dotted throughout *Flaubert's Parrot* are for the most part the coincidences Braithwaite distrusts or the author-ordered parallels drawn between Flaubert and his books, Flaubert and Braithwaite, Braithwaite and Flaubert's books, Ellen Braithwaite and Emma Bovary, Ellen Braithwaite and Louise Colet, and so on.

Art also does not lie but it dissembles in its presentation of truth. Geoffrey Braithwaite is an unreliable narrator but not in the vein of those who set out to mislead; he is not a writer of (published) books, but a doctor, and his book is an assembly of approaches and equivocations, fumblings and graspings. He does not have the answers to very much and even when he advances facts and true accounts he backs away from them shortly afterwards, predisposed to believe that truth lies between facts and fantasies rather than within them. While writing the novel, Barnes noted that ' "Cross Channel" is the story (the longest one, probably) at the centre of the book; the one which is the hinge between the narrator and GF, as between England and France. It's also (at the moment) the one in which the narrator steps forward for the longest period of time.' It is the place also in which Braithwaite's equivocations and vacillations appear most prominently.

The chapter's initial setting is a 'modern ship of fools' (FP, p. 85), the Newhaven to Dieppe ferry, amid the call and response sounds of rattling tables 'like a pair of mechanical birds in a cage' (FP, p. 82). This crossing is out of season, during the 'in-between times, the months that can't make up their minds. Perhaps it's a way of admitting that things can't ever bear the same certainty again' (FP, p. 83). Braithwaite, like Flaubert, is also steeped in irony, another coping mechanism. He rarely arrives at certainty, but instead ferries between different versions, often observing the futility of life and wryly joking about the lack of resolution that surrounds him: 'This is the attraction, and also the danger, of irony: the way it permits a writer to be seemingly absent from his work, yet in fact hintingly present' (FP, p. 87). Braithwaite avoids telling his story as a way of avoiding telling his wife's story, and in recompense distracts himself and the reader with Shandyesque snippets from Flaubert's.

Braithwaite then admonishes modern criticism and modern writers, noting that Flaubert anticipated Roland Barthes's influential essay 'The death of the author' by many decades and that having two endings to a postmodernist novel (as in John Fowles's *The French Lieutenant's Woman*, with its nods to Barthes) is hardly imitating life any better than did the nineteenth-century novel (FP, p. 89), and in fact disingenuously suggests that the reader has a 'choice' when this would occur only if the reader was able to make an informed choice to read one ending alone. It is hard not to conclude that while *Flaubert's Parrot* is a metafictional text it is an anti-postmodernist novel in that its implied author believes in characterisation, causation, and other staples of fiction. Arguably, a case could consequently be made for the view that in the first part of 'Cross channel' the former literary editor in Barnes steps forward and uses Braithwaite as a mouthpiece. Barnes perhaps makes Braithwaite improbably aware of contemporary literary theory, given his background, when for example he describes the twentieth as a 'pragmatic and knowing century' in which 'We no longer believe that language and reality "match up" so congruently' (FP, p. 88), but the vocabulary his narrator employs is never overly technical and his use of language remains in character.

If we take Braithwaite's views as similar to those of Barnes, he does not denigrate or look down upon the practices of the past, such as authorial omniscience (FP, p. 89), but acknowledges that fiction is a historically situated art form shaped by past literary forms and by contemporary social forces, including the increasingly democratic, consumerist forces impacting on authors and readers in postwar society. Before a set of elliptical asterisks, Barnes playfully underlines the metafictional element of his novel with Braithwaite's narration trailing off in a series of hesitations and apologies. He describes himself as a diffident narrator, addressing the reader directly as though a confidante met on the ferry, and thus recalls narrators in such archetypal modernist novels as Albert Camus's *The Fall* and Ford Madox Ford's *The Good Soldier*. Braithwaite adds later in the chapter that 'Nothing much about my character matters' (FP, p. 96), a line paraphrased from *The Good Soldier*, for which Barnes wrote an introduction in 2008.[11] In that introduction, Barnes mentions that Dowell, the narrator of *The Good Soldier*, conjures a picture of himself telling the reader his story beside a fireplace: 'This is a desperate attempt at social and narrative ordinariness. It is not so much that we don't believe the ploy; more that Dowell doesn't have the skill, or the insight, to reduce his tale to a mere fireside yarn. The storyteller isn't up to the level of his own story; he is a bumbler obliged to convey an intrigue of operatic passion which he himself only partially understands.' For Dowell we could read Braithwaite.[12]

The second part of 'Cross channel' focuses on knowing, perceiving and recording the past: 'every so often we are tempted to throw up our hands and declare that history is merely amother literary genre:

the past is autobiographical fiction pretending to be a parliamentary report' (FP, p. 90). Braithwaite wonders about the usefulness of contemporary portraits, written or painted, as ways to perceive the past from the present, and he focuses on the difficulty of using points of comparison (his semi-humorous example is how relative average heights in the nineteenth and twentieth centuries skew judgements about *stature*), as a prelude to considering issues closer to his heart and focused on past and present perceptions of, as well as euphemisms for, madness, adultery, and death. Language, his anecdotes suggest, is indeed no longer thought of as transparent: words are not a window onto reality: 'We look at the sun though smoked glass; we must look at the past though coloured glass' (FP, p. 94).

Braithwaite's imagined interlocutor re-emerges for the chapter's third and final part. Here, in trying to begin to say something about himself Braithwaite is again aware of the reductive nature of description and the straitjacket of form. Personal advertisements provide one model, in which a number of terms and phrases stand for a life: 'No one would think of himself as an active non-smoker inclined to melancholy if that wasn't encouraged, even demanded, by the form' (FP, p. 95). The form additionally requires him to state what he 'seeks', which Braithwaite realises is asking him about companionship, but which also points up the project at the heart of *Flaubert's Parrot*: a search for what? A parrot, truths about Flaubert, the past, art? Or simply a displacement activity filling time, and aimed at avoiding (thoughts of) death? This last is reinforced by an immediate digression into a list of the top ten categories of novel that Braithwaite would ban, which, in their randomness, echo the bewildering classifications of animals in a putative Chinese encyclopaedia cited in Borges's essay 'The analytical language of John Wilkins' and famously discussed by Michel Foucault at the start of his taxonomical study *The Order of Things*. After this list, Braithwaite suddenly veers back into asking once more 'So how do we seize the past?' (FP, p. 100) as though we are to imagine this has been at the back of his mind all this time (which it has, for the entire book, from the first use of this question on p. 14).

Braithwaite uses further discussion of Flaubert as a way to illustrate his views on the past. Explicitly, this images the past as a receding coastline, sometimes seemingly brought into focus by certain lenses, sometimes not. Braithwaite cites Shakespeare on the same page and it is hard not to think that the past for Braithwaite emerges from this as akin to Hamlet's conclusion that 'There is nothing either good or bad, but thinking makes it so' (Act II, sc. ii). Yet, Braithwaite

goes on to justify his approach on the grounds that he believes a knowing, clever obliqueness in writing is preferable to a full-face sincerity
that lacks nuance, subtlety, and an ironic awareness of epistemological polyvalency: 'Does the world progress? Or does it merely shuttle
back and forth like a ferry?' (FP, p. 105). Oscillation and parallax
describe history better than development and supposition and there
are many truths rather than one. Are French customs officers gen-
tlemen and English ones ruffians, Braithwaite wonders? 'I find them
all quite sympathetic, if you treat them properly' (FP, p. 106). This
is true of biography for Braithwaite, where subjects need to be
treated properly in order to make them sympathetic. It is also true
of Flaubert's convoluted story, which Braithwaite tells in a convoluted
way in order to understand better his wife's biography, as he oscillates between aspects of Flaubert's life and his own, finding a closeness missing in his life though his displaced pursuit of the dead, male,
foreign writer.

Finally, we may wonder whether *Flaubert's Parrot* is the only novel
with an examination paper. In it, Braithwaite notes the view of those
who prefer reflection and introspection to the madding crowd and
who therefore 'tend to cite Logan Pearsall Smith: "People say that
life is the thing; but I prefer reading"' (FP, p. 171). As this glib aphorism suggests, through its humour and its leavening of pathos with
bathos, the novel thus approaches some fundamental questions
about the role of the novel in personal and social life: art as religion;
the mystique that attaches to a revered author; and the thrilling aura
of any artefact that, however mistakenly, seems to bring the admirer
a degree or two of separation closer to the 'great writer'. In its treatment of death and 'the life', cultural tourism and the cold hand of
literary criticism, purity and adultery, *Flaubert's Parrot* asks one of
the questions closest to the heart of Barnes's work, where death and
aesthetics coalesce: can art compensate for mortality?

It has been said that *Flaubert's Parrot* 'borrows from the genre of
detective fiction',[13] which is not surprising given Barnes was half-way
through writing the four *Duffy* novels, Martin Amis has been quoted
as saying: 'what [Barnes is] really good at is creating a suspense through
themes and ideas.'[14] This is especially true of *Flaubert's Parrot* but it
is a fair comment on Barnes's oeuvre overall, even though his third
novel is the one reviewers and academics most readily point to when
they wish to discuss him in relation to literary-critical classifications
such as postmodernism or historiographic metafiction. In a review

of Flaubert's letters, Barnes notes that Flaubert felt 'the enduring success of *Madame Bovary* ha[d] skewed, and in his view diminished, public and critical appreciation of his subsequent books';[15] the critical adulation accorded *Flaubert's Parrot* has had a not entirely dissimilar effect on the reception of Barnes's subsequent novels, each of which has had to attempt to fly from under its shadow.

Notes

1 'Julian Barnes in conversation', *Cercles*, 4 (2002), pp. 255–69: p. 259; www.cercles.com.
2 Alison Lee, *Realism and Power: Postmodern British Fiction*, London: Routledge, 1990, p. 1.
3 Barnes's letter to 'Liz'. Unpublished: HRC Barnes holdings Correspondence on *Flaubert's Parrot*.
4 *Trois Contes* is also echoed in one chapter title in *A History of the World in 10½ Chapters*: 'Three simple stories'.
5 For a fuller tracing of Barnes's possible uses of Flaubert see the essay by David Leon Higdon, ' "Unconfessed confessions": the narrators of Graham Swift and Julian Barnes', in James Acheson (ed.), *The British and Irish Novel Since 1960*, London: Macmillan, 1991, 174–91.
6 The holy spirit is of course often represented as a dove, following Luke 3:22 when it descends 'like a dove' on Jesus.
7 Merritt Moseley is making I think only a comparative point, relative to novels that have more overtly metaphorical titles, when he says the book 'really is about Flaubert's parrot' Moseley, *Understanding Julian Barnes*, p. 69.
8 Barnes's letter to 'Liz'. HRC Barnes holdings Correspondence on *Flaubert's Parrot*.
9 Frederick M. Holmes, *The Historical Imagination: Postmodernism and the Treatment of the Past in Contemporary British Fiction*, Victoria: University of Victoria, 1997: p. 11.
10 E. M. Forster, 'Art for art's sake' in *Two Cheers for Democracy*, Harmondsworth: Penguin, 1965, pp. 102–3.
11 Ford Madox Ford, *The Good Soldier*, London: Folio, 2008.
12 See also N. Brooks, 'Interred textuality: the "Good Soldier" and "Flaubert's Parrot" (Ford Madox Ford, Julian Barnes)' in *Critique–Studies in Contemporary Fiction* 41:1 (1999), pp. 45–51.
13 Andrej Gasiorek, *Post-war British Fiction*, London: Edward Arnold, 1995, p. 159.
14 Stout, 'Chameleon novelist', p. 72.
15 Julian Barnes, 'The lost governess', Review of *Gustave Flaubert Correspondance V*, *Times Literary Supplement*, 14 March 2008, pp. 3–5, p. 4.

4

Intricate rented world: *Staring at the Sun*

[It was] some reviewers' expectation that after *Flaubert's Parrot*, his first great success, he would repeat himself by writing 'Victor Hugo's Dachshund'.[1]

Staring at the Sun was possibly to be entitled 'A woman of the century', or 'Question and answer'. Barnes even considered 'The Chinaman's ear', 'Christ/God and the aviator', and 'The only life of Jean Serjeant'. Its final title is shared by a book by the psychiatrist Irvin Yalom, with the subtitle 'Overcoming the terror of death'. The expression's derivation is from the twenty-sixth maxim by the French author François de la Rochefoucauld: 'Neither the sun nor death can be stared at steadily' (*Le soleil ni la mort ne se peuvent regarder fixement*).

Barnes's fourth novel records moments in the life of an ordinary woman, Jean Serjeant, up to a flight she takes in 2021, on which she twice sees the sun setting. The metaphor of the book's title implies that human beings have to stare courageously at the fact of a godless universe: stoically face life as chaotic, but beautiful and marvellous, and death as final, without the consolations offered by religion. The book shares thematic concerns with much of Barnes's other work in its interest in the nature of death and truth; but in this novel the connections with the shape and course of one individual's life are clearer than in most of his writings. Utilising Barnes's favoured tri-partite structure, the novel is divided into three sections situated forty years apart, in the 1940s, 1980s, and 2020s. Thematically, the book moves through a concern with forms of courage: physical, social, and moral. These qualities are principally revealed in the life of Jean Serjeant, who becomes both braver and more intelligent as she gets older, nearing 100 as the book closes. In the book's imagery, Jean is like the mink: tenacious of life.

A prologue also provides one way of approaching the novel's final title. From his cockpit, an airman named Tommy Prosser sees the sunrise over the English Channel one day in June 1941. He then takes his plane down to a lower altitude and finds he sees the sun rise again. This is an ordinary miracle (SS, p. 4) that represents not only a second chance but also the prosaic explanations for seemingly miraculous events. In the first section of the book, set as Jean grows up in the years preceding and including the Second World War, this element of 'ordinary miracles' is represented by the experiences of her favourite uncle Leslie, whose 'miracles' teach her how unusual occurrences that seem magical and mysterious are not so – and may be tricks. Tommy 'Sun-Up' Prosser's story has two follow-ups. The second has been mentioned, when Jean takes flight at the close of the novel, but the first is when Prosser tells his story to a young, impressionable Jean and elaborates on his view of the best way to 'go':

> 'You're climbing straight into the sun because you think that's safe. It's all much brighter than usual up there. You hold your hand up in front of your face and you open your fingers very slightly and squint through them. You carry on climbing. You stare through your fingers at the sun, and you notice that the nearer you get to it, the colder you feel. You ought to worry about this but you don't . . . and you carry on climbing through the thin blue air, staring at the sun through your fingers, frost on your Perspex but all warm inside, all happy and not a thought in your head, until your hand drops in front of you, and then your head drops, and you don't even notice it's curtains . . .' (SS, pp. 31–2)

Jean takes from this a tale of courage but it transpires that her courage and Prosser's are quite different because her choice is to face mortality squarely whereas his is to take the possibility of suicide seriously.

The first of the three Parts begins with Jean reflecting on her ninety-plus years and considering the different forms memory takes: 'Sometimes the past was shot with a hand-held camera; . . . sometimes it eased along, a love story from the silent era, pleasing, out of focus and wholly implausible. And sometimes there was only a succession of stills to be borrowed from the memory' (SS, p. 7). She then recounts her first memory – 'a series of magic lantern slides' – which is of receiving a Christmas present of four hyacinths in a pot at age seven from Uncle Leslie. On later inspection the promised plants turn out to be four upturned golf tees. Jean doesn't lose faith in Leslie though – she believes in people and as a child looks up to Uncle Leslie while everyone else sees him as unreliable and irresponsible.[2] However, she does lose faith in the flowers. As hyacinths in classical mythology represent death and rebirth, this suggests Jean's loss of faith is in an afterlife or resurrection.

Uncle Leslie is one of many men in Jean's life who attempt to influence her, including her grocer father, policeman husband, and insurance clerk son; yet she remains steadfastly independent and this is a significant strand to the book's narrative interest in women's growing independence over the course of the twentieth century. A major touchstone of Part One is Marie Stopes, whose 1918 book *Married Love* is given to Jean by a neighbour in preparation for her marriage to a policeman, Michael Curtis (who comes to represent authority and patriarchy, alluded to by her father's comment that 'You can always trust a policeman', SS, p. 39). The book is not named but passages are reproduced (e.g. SS, p. 41) and reference is made to Stopes's only performed play *Our Ostriches: A play of modern life in three acts* by Marie Carmichael Stopes (1923), with its strong birth-control message.[3] Stopes's subtitle echoes Barnes's structure and its concern with the life of an ordinary modern woman, one whose sexual feeling is unfulfilled by marriage or the temptation of a lesbian affair. Jean is also an unexceptional Gertrude Stein, traveller and pioneer of same-sex relationships. Stein's last words are quoted later in the novel: 'What is the answer?'; when there was no response, she continued 'In that case, what is the question?' (SS, p. 155) Jean has earlier stated her view from the mid-century: 'Women were brought up to believe that men were the answer. They weren't. They weren't even one of the questions' (SS, p. 80).

Further illustrating why the novel was nearly called 'Question and answer', *Staring at the Sun* is full of queries and small puzzles. This first Part poses childhood questions that interest Jean, such as 'why is the mink tenacious of life?'; 'whether there was a sandwich museum?'; 'whether Heaven was up the chimney?' And whether her father was frightened when she and he went for a ride over London in a De Havilland plane (SS, p. 13). All of these questions are directly or indirectly linked to a picture in Jean's bedroom as a girl. This is of a ladder of virtues of the kind advocated in Victorian conduct manuals such as Samuel Smiles's *Self-Help* of 1859 (SS, p. 18). The rungs, in ascending order, are labelled: Industry, Temperance, Prudence, Integrity, Economy, Punctuality, Courage, and Perseverance. Jean understands some of the words and not others. Courage she thinks, means 'going up in aeroplanes'. Seemingly she imagines this because of the stories she is told about the War, which starts when she is 17 and leads Tommy Prosser to be billeted on Jean's family. Prosser, or at least his experience, represents aspiration and wonder in the book's schema, whereas Michael is portrayed as someone who has his feet firmly on the ground, and is thus prosaic, a flat-footed conventional man who keeps Jean from travel and experience.

Part One ends with Jean married and indeed following the conventions of a 'steady life'. She has discussed fear and bravery with Prosser, seen tricks and asked questions with Uncle Leslie, but is now trying to understand sex and contraception with Michael. She considers herself now to have been disabused of her childhood wonder:

> Jean felt that she now knew all the secrets; all the secrets of life. There was a dark, warm cupboard; she had taken out something heavy, wrapped in brown paper. There was no need to cheat – no need to unscrew a tiny viewing-hole and peer in with a torch. She was grown-up. She could carefully and seriously unwrap the paper. She knew what she would find. Four slim ochre points. Golf tees. Of course. What else would you expect? Only a child would take them for hyacinths. Only a child would expect them to sprout. Grown-ups knew that golf tees never sprouted. (SS, p. 66)

Jean's physical courage exists in her forbearance and fortitude alongside other rungs of virtue: ordinary human miracles that are more real than the tricks and magic men have shown her (Part Two begins with the phrase 'Michael struck fire with his heels'). Barnes is therefore interested in the human fascination with supernatural wonders but also with the bravery of an adherence to truth, which leaves Jean without the crutches of illusions she wishes to believe in but finds she cannot.

The novel's second Part moves to the early 1980s, when Jean and Michael have divorced. After twenty years of marriage, Jean 'became, in her own mind, rather anonymous. She wasn't miserable, though she was scarcely happy; she was well enough liked, without joining any of the village's central conspiracies; she was, she slowly decided, rather ordinary' (SS, p. 75). Having become pregnant at 39 (another 'ordinary miracle' because she stopped having her periods at 38, p. 81), Jean has a son, Gregory, whose imminent arrival prompted her to decide to leave Michael and start to live an independent life when seven months pregnant: 'Running away, people said, showed

a lack of courage. Jean wondered if the opposite might be the case'
(SS, p. 80). Unusually for the time, Jean bravely leaves her husband
in the early 1960s to live as a single mother. She therefore predates
second-wave feminism in her quest for independence from a husband who is patronising and traditionally paternalistic. Michael even
strikes her on one occasion (SS, p. 73), situating her perceived faults
in terms of the one signifier 'woman'.

Jean reflects again on the dissimilar 'courage' shown by the sexes,
whose lives traditionally involve different kinds of challenges and fears,
without which there is no bravery: 'Men's courage lay in going out
and nearly getting killed. Women's courage – or so everyone said –
lay in endurance. Men showed courage in violent bouts, women in
patient stretches . . . Then, Jean thought wryly, the men came home
and were bad-tempered, and the women showed courage by enduring their presence' (SS, pp. 78–9). After enduring her unsatisfying
married stability, Jean and her son Gregory move from town to town
'always escaping' from the possibility of pursuit by Michael but also
always searching for greater meaning. Gregory takes to building
model aeroplanes while Jean conceives a plan to visit the Seven
Wonders of the World, revised to suit her own life. Both elements
of the story represent a search for significance and an aspiration towards
truth. On her travels, Jean visits the fifteenth-century 'Temple of
Heaven' in Beijing, bringing to mind her childhood 'ladder of
virtues' that lead to heaven. Here Jean encounters the 'Echo Wall',
suggesting a place and meaning in the book's concerns that would
be akin to the Marabar Caves in E. M. Forster's *A Passage to India*.
The echo wall at the Temple of Heaven implies there are no answers
to ultimate questions, only their echoing enquiry – just as Prosser
would fly upwards alone towards the sun in the sky only to encounter
death, not meaning.

On her trips, Jean remains steadfastly fearless of flying, while her
son Gregory finds that aeroplanes epitomise 'the most infernal conditions in which to die': in certain ignorance of death, claustropho-
bically enclosed, surrounded by strangers and exposed to 'overkill',
multiple sources of death by impact, fire, explosion, exposure and
so forth. Gregory sees it as a 'death that mocks you' (SS, p. 98),
partly because of its faux-domesticity, and this stands in contrast to
Prosser's 'perfect death' flying upwards towards the sun and passing
into unconsciousness with only bright light staring back. Jean's
own personal final Wonder is the Grand Canyon, which 'acted like

a cathedral on religiously inclined tourists, and startlingly argued
without words the power of God and the majesty of his works. Jean's
response was the opposite. The Canyon stunned her into uncertainty'
(SS, p. 100). Jean is unsure if the Canyon means anything: 'If the
Canyon is the question, what is the answer? If the Canyon is the
answer, what is the question? The Canyon, *therefore* . . . ?' (SS, p. 100).
Jean's ordinary miracle here is to see a plane from above, the scale
of the canyon allowing a charter plane to fly along beneath the rim.
Again reminded of the incredible fact of flight, human beings' most
extraordinary achievement, her next visit is to see Tommy Prosser's
widow, from whom she hears of his death in a plane supposedly out
of control and ascending into the sky. Jean reflects on the circumstances and is reminded of Prosser's perfect exit: 'Climbing into
the sun, watching it through slightly parted fingers. The air getting
thinner; the aeroplane skidding about and climbing more slowly. The
patch of frost forming inside the Perspex hood. The gathering cold.
The thinning oxygen. The gradual invasion of contentment, then of
joy. The slowness; the happy slowness of it all' (SS, 107). Prosser
emerges in her imagination as a slightly crazed airman who, out
of courage or cowardice, chose the nature of his own death, but is
otherwise less than the war hero Jean might have wished.

Of growing importance in the book's exploration of ordinary
courage, Jean's son Gregory is a withdrawn child who is both pas-
sive and pragmatic by nature. He lives with his mother and does
not marry; he works in an insurance office and does not travel. To
Gregory, not Prosser but a figure called Cadman the aviator is a touchstone for the escapism of flight and courage in the face of death (SS,
p. 112). Robert Cadman was a real-life eighteenth-century folk hero:
a steeplejack and professional tightrope walker most famous for slid-
ing down a rope while blowing a trumpet from the cupola of St Paul's
Cathedral, winning him the nickname 'Icarus of the rope.' Cadman
met his death in 1739 at St Mary's Church, Shrewsbury, where there
is a tablet commemorating his attempt to fly from the top of the tower
across the River Severn along 250 metres of rope, to which he was
attached. Because of the plaque's reference to flying, Barnes has it
in *Staring at the Sun* that Cadman built a pair of wings and launched
himself to fly over the River, but the rope snapped and Cadman fell
to his death half-way across. Gregory decides that Cadman's body fell
but at the same time his soul rose and flew, according to the epitaph
on the plaque: ''Twas not for want of skill; / Or Courage, to perform

the task, he fell: / No, no – a faulty cord, being drawn too tight, /
Hurry'd his soul on high to take her flight, / Which bid the body
here beneath good night.' Gregory thinks that the story implies that
God rewards the brave with eternal life and 'If so – if Heaven was
gained by courage – then Gregory didn't rate his chances' (SS, p. 113).

Aside from news of the death of Uncle Leslie, the other key
narrative element of Part Two is Jean's relationship with Rachel, a
militant feminist. An unlikely girlfriend of Gregory's, Rachel makes
a pass at Jean, who she says is 'still waiting for some man to come
along and answer all the questions' (SS, p. 124). Rachel is an
assertive, forthright character who takes for granted the hold on life
that Jean, from an older generation, has had to struggle for. This marks
the end of what Jean thinks of as ancient times, or 'Asian times' after
her Chinese visit, which are associated with male rule, dominated by
figures like Prosser, Michael, and Uncle Leslie, for whom the world
has been designed according to Rachel: 'And when you asked them
the simplest questions . . . they would not answer. They pretended there
was something wrong with the question. That is not a real question.
Why do you ask such a thing? There is no answer because there is
no question' (SS, p. 137).

Part Three, set in the future, envisions a time when life is further
dominated by the catechism of questions and answers, but the context has altered and the source of potential answers has changed.
Now, ethical and moral questions take over from the social ones that
dominated Part Two concerning freedom and feminism, marriage
and motherhood. Jean's initial question of Part Three derives from
Uncle Leslie's death – how do you tell a good life from a bad life?
To Gregory, Leslie's is a brave death and he is impressed by his great
uncle's spirit and behaviour on his final visit. Jean notes that there's
'no bravery without fear' (SS, p. 130) but that 'a good death was any
death not swamped by agony, fear and protest' (SS, p. 136). Jean is
now 99 years old and Gregory is 60; they are both exercised by questions of mortality and Jean reflects on the fact that she is now 'the
mother of an old man' (SS, p. 143). Since the first decade of the new
century Gregory's thoughts have turned to suicide amidst a wave of
self-killing among the elderly as part of a movement to gain better
conditions for old people (militant gerontology having replaced the
militant feminism of Part Two). These questions of the good life and
death are the ones that come to be explored by Gregory via the General
Purposes Computer (GPC).[4] Begun in 1998, GPC is a state-sponsored

program that allows people to ask any kind of factual or conjectural question that is information-centred, organised in subject categories. Containing 'All things known to people' the Computer finally goes on-line in 2003 and is accessible from municipal GPCHQs: 'You keyed in your social security number, and output was modified to your level of understanding' (SS, p. 147). As from 2008, a new level that can be requested is The Absolute Truth (TAT), and this is what Gregory asks permission for in the central pages of Part Three.

TAT's answers are said to be clearly but poetically expressed, and they give an existential truth. Jean is sceptical about the machine and believes the 'serious questions always remained unanswered' (SS, p. 153) After a life of questioning, this becomes her position of moral courage, living without answers beyond those she can decide upon for herself. Her stance is not something Gregory can easily live with, and he bombards GPC with questions about how others have died. At one point, Gregory is told the maxim from La Rochefoucauld that gives the book its title, and he relays this to Jean. She replies:

> 'You *can* stare at the sun. Twenty years before you were born I knew someone who learned to stare at the sun . . . He was a pilot. He had to learn about the sun. After a while you can get used to it. You just have to look at it through parted fingers; then you can manage. You can stare at the sun for as long as you like.' Perhaps, she thought, after a while you begin to grow webbing between your fingers. (SS, p. 157)

Jean has learned more from Prosser's anecdote than she has from 'Asian Times', the answers provided by a patriarchal culture that has provided facts and information but no answers to the 'real' questions. Jean thinks Gregory is 'screaming at the sky':

> it was just a grown-up way of doing what she and Uncle Leslie had done nearly a century ago beyond the smelly beeches at the dogleg fourteenth. Putting your head back and roaring at the empty heavens, knowing that however much noise you made, nobody up there would hear you. And then you flopped down on your back, exhausted, self-conscious and a little pleased: even if no one was listening, you had somehow made your point. (SS, p. 159)

Jean hopes that this will be enough for Gregory and that his fall back to earth will not be too painful. Meanwhile her son pursues Answers by attempting to frame the best Questions of TAT. However, Gregory's quizzing of GPC only leads him to formulate 14 possibilities concerning God's existence or non-existence, ending with speculations that the world is a flawed first draft or that God had 'destroyed himself at the beginning of time' (SS, p. 166). Gregory also ponders whether it is more courageous to believe or not believe in God.[5]

Following this line of questioning, Gregory now quizzes TAT about fears of death and whether they are eradicable. He learns that near-death experiences (NDEs) have released many people from death anxiety and there is now a clinical procedure to induce an NDE, which may or may not work for Gregory. He refuses this but conjectures, in a sentence that prefigures the final chapter of Barnes's next book, *A History of the World in 10½ Chapters*, that 'there might be a life everlasting so designed that you soon began to long for unattainable death: in other words, the reverse of that daily human condition in which you feared death and longed for unattainable life everlasting' (SS, p. 179).

By contrast, having visited her Seven Wonders of the World, Jean compiles a list of the 'seven private wonders of life': not rungs on the 'ladder of virtue' but ordinary miracles from birth to death that mark the progression of a life's stages. In general, Jean feels she has been unaware or unconscious of these events, which for the most part have happened to her:

> Most people didn't do anything: that was the truth. You are brought up on heroism and drama, on Tommy Prosser hurtling through a world of black and red; you are allowed to think that adult life consists of a constant exercise of personal will; but . . . Most of life is passive, the present a pinprick between an invented past and an imagined future. She had done little in her time; Gregory had done less. (SS, pp. 183–4)

Jean's latest expression of courage is to look at the reality of approaching death steadily and bravely: in answer to Gregory's direct questions, she gives him *her absolute truth* that death is final, religion is nonsense, and suicide is not permissible (SS, p. 187). These are not erudite answers, but it is made clear that they need not be when Gregory is told the quotation from Kierkegaard that heads Part Three: 'Immortality is no learned question' (SS, p. 188).

Jean's sign of valour and ordinary heroism is to face the facts of existence truthfully, without what Barnes would see as the false promises of God and an afterlife; yet, her absence of faith is not a choice on Jean's part. 'Perhaps faith was like night vision', she concludes, thinking of Prosser, 'He wouldn't be aware that something was wrong; he just wouldn't be able to see anything. Maybe faith was like that; either they'd fitted the right instrument panel or they hadn't. It was a design feature, a capacity; nothing to do with knowledge or intelligence or perceptiveness' (SS, p. 191). But neither Jean nor Gregory is fitted with faith, leaving them instead with their own truths. And while Gregory finds it hard to be brave in the face of these truths, Jean has greater reserves of courage and her fortitude is presented as Barnes's ordinary human miracle in the knowledge of eternal oblivion. This is underlined by their different understanding of Leslie's death, which Gregory continues to believe was a good one, but which Jean knows 'had oscillated between pure anger and pure fear' in his final hours (SS, p. 193). It may still have been a good death she decides because greater courage may exist in faking forbearance for others than in maintaining it privately. The novel concludes with Jean deciding on one last journey for herself before death, which is a re-enactment of Prosser's experience from the prologue, but at sunset not sunrise. Gregory accompanies her and while the incident brings him to tears she greets the dying sun 'face to face', smiling 'towards this postmortal phosphorescence' of the sun's final glow as it disappears below the horizon.

In one respect, *Staring at the Sun* is the story of one unexceptional woman's personal and social courage over the course of a century. In another respect, the book is a meditation on the twentieth century's central existential question of suicide in an absurd world. While this is a question of courage that eats away at Gregory, it is not a genuine option for Jean who chooses to experience life on her own terms, constructing in the end personal answers to the difficult questions of life. She stares at the reality of Philip Larkin's 'Aubade', greeting the sunrise as well as the sunset of what he calls in that poem an 'Intricate rented world' without either a physical heaven 'up the chimney', as she thought as a child, or the Temple of Heaven promised by society in a loving family, or the religious heaven that could be a consolation near death.

Staring at the Sun tells a life story in three parts or stages. By focusing on youth, the prime of life and old age, Barnes gives a picture of a largely uneventful existence that is unremarkable but none the less worth living. Jean's disappointments, starting with Uncle Leslie's early tricks, are balanced by joys and moments of discovery leading to the enlightenment of personal enfranchisement. Jean Serjeant is not portrayed as brilliant or gifted but her courage lies in choosing her own life in the face of both the social pressures on women to conform and the unanswered questions of mortality.

Notes

1 Moseley, 'Julian Barnes', pp. 27–37. Moseley is referring to a comment made by Barnes in this interview: Amanda Smith, 'Julian Barnes', *Publisher's Weekly*, 236:18 (3 November 1989), pp. 73–4.
2 Leslie also reveals an unexplored anti-Semitic prejudice in his aside that 'your jew doesn't really enjoy golf'. This would seem to be social observation on Barnes's part, as he observes that, for example, his parents 'had the low-level anti-Semitism of their time and class' (NF, p. 13).
3 Stopes also wrote several other plays, including one on the need for sex education entitled *Vectia*, which was banned by the Lord Chamberlain. The 1918 text of *Married Love* can be found at: http://digital.library.upenn.edu/women/stopes/married/1918.html (accessed 16 November 2009).
4 The name echoes the title 'General Purposes Committee': a common name for a group that has oversight of all matters not explicitly dealt with elsewhere in an organisation or government.
5 This is further discussed in Barnes's memoir *Nothing to Be Frightened of* (NF, p. 191), where it is additionally speculated that God might be an ironist.

5

Safe for love: *A History of the World in 10½ Chapters*

> And so it is with love. We must believe in it . . . If we don't, then we merely surrender to the history of the world and to someone else's truth.
>
> HW, p. 246.

A series of unofficial or unauthorised versions, Barnes's fourth novel has love as its chief stowaway. Love, which intrudes into this book most conspicuously in its half-chapter, opposes history and orthodoxy because its story is individual and personal, though not necessarily happy. Love may be marginalised in old and current 'news', but it is a motivating, directing, inspiring force which stops history from being absurd. Barnes focuses on romantic love, but other forms of love, particularly familial, are amenable to similar deployment as forces that history largely overlooks, but without which there would be no humanity.

> I can tell you why to love. Because the history of the world, which only stops at the half-house of love to bulldoze it into rubble, is ridiculous without it. The history of the world becomes brutally self-important without love. Our random mutation is essential because it is unnecessary.
> (HW, p. 240)

He goes on to say that 'Love won't change the history of the world' but what it can do is subvert it, undermine it, challenge it. This is the thrust of one of the main arguments running through *A History of the World in 10½ Chapters*, where love is seen to be at best ignored and at worst bludgeoned by history. To protest this fact is one of the main purposes of the book's half-chapter, and is echoed in a sentiment expressed in Barnes's next novel: 'I want to make the world safe for love' (TO, p. 221).

Humour also courses through the stories in *A History of the World in 10½ Chapters*, undermining attempts to treat history in coherent ways as monolithic or even to read Barnes's book as a unified work. *A History of the World in 10½ Chapters* is not a historical novel but is both a novel about history and a series of generic experiments patched together; it stands as a comment on history within the discipline of the comic novel, and so, while it should not be taken too lightly as an entertainment, it should also not be taken too seriously as expressing any overall thesis. The impact of the book rests on a multiplicity of voices, perspectives, and truths, implying that there are commonalities between disparate human experiences and events but also a diversity of ways of telling stories. It purports to argue that truth lies in the need to believe in illusions such as free will, that survival resides in the need to love despite the failures of love, and that objective history rests on the need for collective silence over the certainty of fallacy. Above all in the book's observations on Western society is the human need for narrative: for stories that contain truth without necessarily telling the truth, like fiction. In *Love, etc* Barnes thus has his hyper-articulate part-surrogate Oliver say 'What is human tragedy for today's diminished species? To act as if we have free will while knowing we don't' (LE, p. 197).

Barnes decides in *Flaubert's Parrot* that there's a temptation to see history as 'merely another literary genre', autobiography masquerading as a 'parliamentary report' (FP, p. 90). In his fifth novel we have this idea brought to fruition as ten diverse fragments and a parenthetical address to the reader present a world history that can be nothing of the sort but can be a connected series of stories. Barnes notes in interview how history is necessarily selective because the vast majority of events go unrecorded and that it is also 'literary' whenever it departs from a simple description of facts.[1]

Alongside *Flaubert's Parrot*, *A History of the World in 10½ Chapters* is Barnes's most experimental work; one which illustrates the thesis of Roland Barthes's essay 'From work to text': e.g. '[T]he Text . . . cannot be apprehended as part of a hierarchy or even a simple division of genres. What constitutes the Text is, on the contrary (or precisely), its subversive force with regard to old classifications . . . If the Text raises problems of classification, that is because it always implies an experience of limits.'[2] Lying in many people's opinion somewhere between a novel and a collection of interlinked short stories, *A History of the World in 10½ Chapters* has been criticised for being both arbitrarily piecemeal and unrepresentatively Eurocentric, yet the title at least pointedly and jokily advertises it not as *the* history but *a* history of the world. Barnes's retorts to his objectors are incorporated in the book itself, which implies that historiography is always partial and selective: it is not complete and comprehensive but fragmentary, told from a point of view, and subject to the author's theories, in-fills, and prejudices as well as the narrative features of story-telling. Indeed, *A History of the World* contains its own commentary: 'The history of the world? Just voices echoing in the dark; . . . stories, old stories that sometimes seem to overlap; strange links, impertinent connections' (HW, p. 242). Barnes has said that against history bear-ing down on the individual can be put three things: religion, art, and love. Religion, he thinks, is not true, art does not satisfy everyone, and so love is the final 'fall-back position'. By contrast, history is seen as impersonal; it leaves out the most important human elements – faith, aesthetics, affect – and its march of progress, power, and politics leaves many casualties: 'when love fails, we should blame the history of the world. If only it had left us alone, we could have been happy' (HW, p. 246).

This last sentence reveals the element in human history that drives Barnes's novel: free will. Obscuring the alternatives occasioned by different possible choices, most histories almost inevitably impart a linear understanding of a seemingly preordained connected series of events that culminates in an endpoint retrospectively selected by the writer. By contrast, the element of free will is pointed up most fully in the final chapter of Barnes's novel, 'The dream', which explores a consumerist heaven in which everything the individual desires can be chosen. Earlier chapters have shown the competition between out-side forces (God, the Church, doctors, oppressive political regimes, film directors, terrorists) to influence both individual behaviour and the course of history alongside counterforces born of subjective pref-erence and happenstance. Subversion at the margins of history is arguably much closer to a description of Barnes's text, which has choice, chance, chaos, and catastrophe undermining the best laid plans.

A section of the novel central to a discussion of its meanings is 'Parenthesis'. This is understood to be the title's half-chapter because the contents page accords it no number while the others are annotated from one to ten. Yet its status is complex and intriguing. It is a half-chapter, and a parenthesis, to suggest that it both sits within and outside the novel: to use an analogy with drama, it is an 'aside' to the audience by the author as narrator. Additionally, its introduction of titular levity into the otherwise oppressive gravity of such a Herculean undertaking as 'a history of the world' is indicated by its absurdity, which itself points to the absurdity of a definitive global history.

Is a half-chapter unfinished or missing another half, or is it something else altogether? The term provokes comparison with other expressions: a half-truth for example, or the choice of whether to understand a glass as half-full or half-empty. In other words, it seems that a half-chapter is not the full story and does not pretend to be. Here, it is an essay, which is to say an attempt as opposed to an account. Yet, the intrusion of the (unnamed) authorial voice arguably creates a hierarchy of discourse privileging this half-narrative over the other stories. The half-chapter is marginal but also central, just as the woodworm's narration of the Ark story in the first story 'The stowaway' privileges it over that of all the other animals, including Noah.

And if the half-chapter is a 'Parenthesis', is it inserted as explanation or afterthought or neither? It could be understood as an alternative or addition both to the Marxist Hegelian theory of history as dialectic (of thesis, antithesis, and synthesis) and to such approaches as the historical materialism of Walter Benjamin's 'Theses on the philosophy of history'. In the fourteenth of his theses, Benjamin writes that 'History is the subject of a structure whose site is not homogenous, empty time, but time filled by the presence of the now'. Against these dictates of the present writing its own past, inhabiting history, Barnes's parenthesis, a thesis in brackets, seeks to be outside of time in its invocation and evocation of love as 'some tardy addition to the agenda. It reminds me of those half-houses which according to normal criteria of map reading shouldn't exist' (HW, p. 236).

In terms of the novel overall, these half-houses, half-chapters, and half-truths figure in the subversive approach taken to history in each of the stories, where the relationship is exposed between power (especially ecclesiastical and doctrinal) and 'being in the true', in Foucauldian terms. Each chapter has its counter-presence speaking against authority from the woodworm to Kath Ferris in 'The survivor' or the competing accounts of the Raft of the Medusa in 'Shipwreck'. The novel's essentially parodic tone punctures official discourse and revels in bathos as one dominant account after another is mocked by the perspective and presence of the marginalised, on the Ark or the Titanic, in the South American jungle or in the story of Jonah's

Whale: 'As in most of the Old Testament, there's a crippling lack
of free will around – or even the illusion of free will' (HW, p. 176).
This is picked up in 'The mountain', a story of nineteenth-century
'faith': of belief in religion versus belief in evolution. Set initially
near Dublin in 1837, the year Victoria became Queen of Britain and
Ireland, it concerns a daughter's pilgrimage to Mount Ararat, the
supposed resting-place of the Ark.[3] While her dying father deems
Genesis to contain nothing more substantial than 'the Myth of the
Deluge', Miss Fergusson believes in the 'reality of Noah's Ark'; she
also now considers her father's inability many years earlier to see beauty
in Géricault's painting of 'The Raft of the Medusa' to be paralleled
by his failure to recognise God's 'eternal design, and its essential
goodness' when the 'proof of this plan and of this benevolence lay
manifest in Nature, which was provided by God for Man's enjoyment'
(HW, p. 147). In 1839, Miss Fergusson intends to 'intercede for the
soul of [her] father' at the monastery on Ararat (HW, p. 149). Her
mission ends in disaster but this matters less than the fact that the
motivation for her pilgrimage is founded in God-given human free
choice: 'There always appear to be two explanations of everything. That
is why we have been given free will, in order that we may choose the
correct one. My father failed to comprehend that his explanations were
based as much upon faith as mine. Faith in nothing' (HW, p. 154).
This is in outline an example of Pascal's wager, a rational argument
for religious faith: since the individual does not know for certain
whether or not God exists, it is logical to believe, because the possible
consequences of believing in God are salvation or mere self-deception,
whereas the likely outcomes of not believing in God's existence are
damnation if He does exist and oblivion if He doesn't.

Faith is therefore for Miss Fergusson seemingly an exercise of will
against believing in nothing. Her companion on Mount Ararat, Miss
Logan, is consequently left wondering whether Miss Fergusson does
not finally *choose* to take a leap of faith:

> The question she was avoiding was whether Miss Fergusson might not
> have been the instrument of her own precipitation, in order to achieve
> or confirm whatever it was she wanted to achieve or confirm. Miss
> Fergusson had maintained, when they first stood before the haloed moun-
> tain, that there were two explanations of everything, that each required
> the exercise of faith, and that we had been given free will in order that
> we might choose between them. This dilemma was to preoccupy Miss
> Logan for years to come. (HW, p. 168)

Reminiscent of the catechistic emphasis on question and answer in
Barnes's previous novel, this end to 'The mountain' sits alongside
the other unanswered questions in the book, such as whether or not
Kath Ferris's doctors are real, and the questions answered only for
the reader, such as whether Franklin Hughes struck a deal with 'The
visitors'. Another of Barnes's points emphasised here is the fact that
human decisions are often based not on reason but on drives such as
faith, implying that the historian's task of establishing causation and
motivation must often be based not on evidence but on supposition.

'You aren't too good with the truth, either, your species. You keep
forgetting things, or you pretend to' (HW, p. 29). This is the conclusion of the first narrator in Barnes's book, which recognises that
the world needs defamiliarising if the reader is to think anew about
history. Humans blame others according to the woodworm: 'that's
always your first instinct. And if you can't blame someone else, then
start claiming the problem isn't a problem anyway' (HW, p. 29). Seen
through the eyes of the woodworm narrator, human historical arguments appear primarily to be wilful accounts that lay down what the
authors want to believe and leave out what they want to forget. 'The
stowaway' uses the account of the Flood from Genesis (8:4) as a point
of origin for all existing life now on the planet: a primal narrative of
survival, of debates between story and history, religion and science,
human and animal perspectives, authorised and alternative versions,
choices over the clean and the unclean. It initiates the images of
extinction, endurance, and (un)natural selection that run through the
remaining chapters in its focus on the fates of the woodworm and
the Behemoth; it also suggests humanity's inability to see different
sides to events and people's propensity for intoxication and delusion.
These are the drivers of history, as explained later in the novel in
'Parenthesis': 'We make up a story to cover the facts we don't know
or can't accept; we keep a few true facts and spin a new story round
them. Our panic and our pain are only eased by soothing fabulation;
we call it history' (HW, p. 242, echoing p. 109). As I noted in the
Introduction, Barnes glosses fabulation in interview as

> a medical term for what you do when a lot of your brain has been
> destroyed either by a stroke or by alcoholism, or that sort of thing. And
> – it's rather gratifying for the novelist – the human mind can't exist
> without the illusion of a full story. So it fabulates and it convinces itself
> that the fabulation is as true and concrete as what it 'really' knows. Then
> it coherently links the real and the totally imagined in a plausible
> narrative.[4]

In effect, 'The stowaway' takes a founding myth of religious belief and suggests that the only orthodox narrative of it we have, the word of God passed down through Moses, is not a single, true account but an interested, partial one.[5] A different narrator, an unofficial, even fugitive one, gives a widely divergent account. Barnes also sets up his narrating woodworm as the one character who appears across the stories. Teasing those who would assert that a long piece of prose fiction without at least one character featuring consistently is not a novel, Barnes inserts this bookworm as a figure who pops up throughout the narrative as though eating its way through the course of human histor(iograph)y. It is perhaps the worm of conscience reminding us that 'reality' is often myth: 'For the point is this: not that myth refers us back to some original event which has been fancifully transcribed as it passed through the collective memory; but that it refers us forward to something that will happen, that must happen. Myth will become reality, however sceptical we might be' (HW, p. 181). This is a message in 'Three simple stories' suggesting that myth points not backward but forward ('The mountain' was earlier to be titled 'Backwards and forwards'), because it expresses a truth and describes something that will happen one day in a form that will be believed (the essence of the myth of Jonah and the Whale will happen in another story).[6] The crucial element here is belief. 'My account you can trust', says the woodworm (HW, p. 4). Do we trust the teller and not the tale? On the story of a man in the late nineteenth-century, James Bartley, surviving half a day in the belly of a whale, Barnes says he believes it, though modern scientists don't. 'You may not credit it, but what has happened is the story has been retold, adjusted, updated; it has shuffled nearer. For Jonah now read Bartley. And one day there will be a case, one which even you will believe . . . And then people will believe the myth of Bartley, which was begotten by the myth of Jonah' (HW, p. 181). This seems simply an act of faith but it is also a process of mutation and natural selection: the story survives by adaptation.

Anticipating the farcical debate in 'The wars of religion', 'The stowaway' concentrates upon that which supposedly separates humans from animals, 'discourse of reason', and proceeds to explore the abuses to which the faculty of logic can be put, creating facts, arguments, and historical beliefs that are both ludicrous and erroneous. The following story, 'The visitors', considers both the competing narratives of history that humans fight over and the gaps in the historical record: the unrecorded, unsubstantiated, unwitnessed, and unknown. To the

guests on the *Santa Euphemia* cruise ship, including his girlfriend,
Hughes appears a collaborator, such that when the American Special
Forces raid the ship: 'there remained no witness to corroborate
Franklin Hughes's story of the bargain he had struck with the Arabs'
(HW, p. 58). In the face of what appears to be the evidence, Hughes's
own version is assumed to be another self-interested oration and even
his girlfriend, 'who had become Irish for a few hours without real-
izing it', never speaks to him again. Only the chapter's third-person
narrator knows and tells 'the truth', reminding the reader of the artifice
that is omniscient narration.

In the fourth chapter, 'The survivor', Kath Ferris considers official
accounts of the past to be a male bastion of dates and battles against
which she posits the belief that history – memory and truth – is in
the mind.[7] Kath believes she is constructing a thought-dialogue as a
survival mechanism while she drifts the ocean, replaying conversations with Greg: 'everything's connected, isn't it, and women are more
closely connected to all the cycles of nature and birth and rebirth on
the planet than men, who are only impregnators after all' (HW, p. 89).
Here Barnes pitches understandings of masculine and feminine
principles against one another (aggression against creation, conviction against intuition), positing twin human forces of destruction and
survival. Within the story, there is both an assertion of the cyclical,
connected nature of human reality, like a Ferris wheel, and an
impulse to break the cycle: 'The mind got carried away, she found
herself repeating. Everything was connected, the weapons and the nightmares. That's why they'd had to break the cycle. Start making things
simple again. Begin at the beginning. People said you couldn't turn
the clock back, but you could. The future was in the past' (HW,
p. 104). The doctors' version of events is different: they maintain that
Kath was found off Darwin, going round in circles in her boat, and
hallucinating: 'You mustn't fool yourself . . . We've got to look at things
how they are; we can't rely on fabulation any more. It's the only way
we'll survive' (HW, p. 111). Comparable to, for example, the woodworm's story in 'The stowaway', or Miss Fergusson's father's dismissal
of religion in 'The mountain', 'The survivor' is a story of Darwinism
against religious belief. Kath sets off from Darwin, the choice of name
on Barnes's part hinting at her fitness for survival, and it is her adaptation, progressing beyond a rapacious, destructive male world, that
brings her and her two cats, who become seven, to be the latest Ark
survivors.

In 'Shipwreck' the book's rhetorical inquiry into history focuses on
the need to transcribe and ritualise calamity, which is an image of the
larger impulse to turn life into story: 'How do you turn catastrophe
into art?' (HW, p. 125) This is a particularly pertinent question because
of the floods, earthquakes, drownings, persecutions, and deaths that
suffuse the book's narratives, each of which carries the taint of disaster in one form or another (imaged in the deathwatch beetle as
opposed to the woodworm that represents survival). The answer to
the question of why, if not how, is offered by the narrator:

> We have to understand it, of course, this catastrophe; to understand it,
> we have to imagine it, so we need the imaginative arts. But we also need
> to justify it and forgive it, this catastrophe, however minimally. Why
> did it happen, this mad act of Nature, this crazed human moment? Well,
> at least it produced art. Perhaps, in the end, that's what catastrophe is
> *for.* (HW, p. 125)

The succeeding discussion is reminiscent of *Flaubert's Parrot*: it
contains three responses to the actual painting, preceded by eight alternative moments the painter might have chosen, with eight accom-
panying notes explaining the pros and cons of each possibility, none
of which Géricault selected: 'the painting which survives is the one
that outlives its own story. Religion decays, the icon remains; a narrative is forgotten, yet its representation still magnetizes' (HW, p. 133).
Such is also the view to which Chris and Toni subscribe during their
National Gallery experiments in *Metroland*, though they expected to
be able to record the visible signs of people being magnetized.

Barnes expands the answer to his question after he has described
and discussed the scene(s) that Géricault did and did not paint. 'We
are all lost at sea, washed between hope and despair, hailing something that may never come to rescue us. Catastrophe has become art;
but this is no reducing process. It is freeing, enlarging, explaining.
Catastrophe has become art: that is, after all, what it is for' (HW,
p. 137). Barnes tries to amplify this point by discussing the Ark
further. And particularly the shift, precipitated by Michelangelo, in
fine art's preferred way of representing the flood: 'What fills the foreground are the anguished figures of those doomed antediluvians
left to perish when the chosen Noah and his family were saved. The
emphasis is on the lost, the abandoned, the discarded sinners, God's
detritus' (HW, p. 138). The point here for the novel is that modern
art is more often concerned with tragedy, even if history prefers the
march of progress, emphasising the triumph of the victors.

Among other aspects of historical distortion, 'Upstream!' focuses on the perils of representation; of simulation and dissimulation (using the tribespeople whom the missionaries sought to convert as extras), verisimilitude and dissemblance: the relation between what is 'real' and what is 'false' in the context of cultural difference. The narrator Charlie makes great play of his team-effort but is deeply egocentric as the film crew try to get the actors and the action upstream, imitating the life-struggle of sperm or those on the other rafts, boats, arks and missions in the novel. In this, 'Upstream!' also exemplifies the tension between individual and collective effort and goals as Charlie fabulates his own story in piecemeal fashion, sending letters from one imitation of life to another, universalising his film's story-line: 'it's about the sort of conflict running through human life in every time and every civilization' (HW, p. 208). This is a trite statement that may be true for Charlie within his story but is also pertinent for Barnes as he constructs another narrative of survival framed by deception, cultural conflict, representation, and a one-sided version of events. Charlie's unrequited love letters are followed by Barnes's own meditations on the importance of love in 'Parenthesis', which is inserted as a counter-history, particularly opposing the grand narratives of the kind Charlie feels his film is about: 'How great ideas like the Church get bogged down in bureaucracy. How Christianity starts off as the religion of peace but ends up violent like other religions. You could say the same about Communism or anything else, any big idea' (HW, p. 208).

Chapter 9, 'Project Ararat', exemplifies the conclusion of the first tale of the *Titanic* in 'Three simple stories': 'Marx's elaboration of Hegel: history repeats itself, the first time as tragedy, the second time as farce' (HW, p. 175). Where Miss Fergusson's story in 'The mountain' ended in tragedy with her death on Ararat, Tiggler's ends in farce and the launch of a second Project Ararat; but the comical tone of the novel undercuts pretensions towards grand theories of historical patterning. Significantly, however, the chapter starts and ends in the second person, inserting the reader, positioned on an island ferry, into the narrative in a way that brings to mind the comment on history's supposed forward march from *Flaubert's Parrot*: 'Does the world progress? Or does it merely shuttle back and forth like a ferry?' (FP, p. 105).

Finally, 'The dream' satirises for the secular mind the endless repetitions suggested by the concept of an afterlife progressing life's journey into eternity: the tediousness and banality of unchanging paradise with no future, or even catastrophe, to bring newness into the world, while still having an eternity to 'survive'. In 'The survivor', which was to be the book's penultimate chapter until quite close to publication, Kath Ferris asks: 'Bad dreams. Nightmares, I suppose. When does a dream become a nightmare? These dreams of mine go on after I've woken up. It's like having a hangover. The bad dreams won't let the rest of life go on' (HW, p. 94). Presented as a Utopian vision that becomes a banality if not a nightmare, 'The dream' asserts the importance for human beings of both a struggle against possible failure and a belief in endings – history provides the only templates for human visions of paradise. It is therefore a critique not of 'Heaven', whatever that could be, but of the human ability to imagine utopia. This, Barnes says, is modern democratic heaven: we give them more of life, that's all they ask for nowadays. In other words, Heaven is presented as yet another flawed stratagem for survival.

The struggle for survival, the pursuit of a better Ark, is positioned as the driving force of life in Barnes's novel, which is a series of narratives largely predicated upon self-preservation motivated by exclusion and persecution of others. More of life without more variety seems a tedious prospect but more of love would seem to be what Barnes wishes for the world, like many authors before him, from Auden to Larkin. In the parenthetical nocturnal musing of Barnes's half-chapter, love protects the individual from loneliness, placing a pair in the ark of survival, but more importantly love has the most potential to be a counter to the predatory forces of exclusion and per-secution, often placing at least one other before the self; and though it fails 'we must believe in love, just as we must believe in free will and objective truth' (HW, p. 246). Barnes is content to frame his com-ments as an insomniac's truth, spoken while lying beside his lover, knowing they will seem different in the cold light of day. These three necessary self-deceptions are however the ones by which Barnes seems to argue each individual must live: this is his subjective truth in the novel. And *A History of the World* is a subjective view of his-tory, within which love is inserted as the only hope of survival, free will figures as an escape from determinism, and 'objective truth' avoids the descent into relativism. These are beliefs of the less-deceived, Barnes might argue.

Given Barnes's dominant view, that life and history are broadly cyclical and repetitious, with variations, the title of *A History of the*

World begins to signify further. It is a representative story, as fiction
– rather than history – often purports to be, telling an individual and
specific story that has universal resonance. Here, not history but the
pretensions of writing history come under closer scrutiny. Barnes's
book aspires to the status not of historiography but of myth and in
this its argument might be that historians could profitably attempt
something similar in their aims: to come clean about the fact that
they are often telling the story of what might have happened rather
than what did. Kath Ferris speaks for fiction here, in opposition to
traditional masculinised history:

> They say I don't understand things. They say I'm not making the right
> connections. Listen to them, listen to them and their connections. This
> happened, they say, and as a consequence that happened. There was a
> battle here, a war there, a king was deposed, famous men – always famous
> men, I'm sick of famous men – made events happen. Maybe I've been
> out in the sun too long, but I can't see their connections. I look at the
> history of the world, which they don't seem to realize is coming to an
> end, and I don't see what they see. (HW, p. 97)

Barnes's novel was published in 1989. That was indeed a year in which
history was thought to come to an end according to one hypothesis.
At least until the events of September 2001 in New York, for some
writers in the West an apparent 'End of History' occurred with the
closing stages of the Cold War, the Tiananmen Square protests and
the fall of the Berlin Wall in 1989, followed by the growth of glob-
alisation, proclaimed by the neoconservative Francis Fukuyama as the
triumph of economic liberalism. This turn in ideological power in
Europe, a Western-welcomed Eastern revolution, would be treated
in what may seem the most unexpected book of Barnes's unusual
literary career. But before we turn to 1992's *The Porcupine*, there are
another two books to discuss, or, as the first and second parts of a
novel-sequence of two, perhaps they are two half-books.

Notes

1 See Guignery ' "History in question(s)" ', p. 53.
2 Roland Barthes, 'From work to text' in Josue V. Harari (ed.), *Textual
   Strategies*, Ithaca: Cornell University Press, 1979, pp. 73–81, p. 75.
3 Barnes gained information about the display of the Raft in Dublin from
   Lee Johnson's 'The "Raft of the Medusa" in Great Britain', *Burlington
   Magazine* XCVI (August 1954), pp. 249–54. An article that opens up the

history of the competing versions of Géricault's painting that went on tour in Europe is Christine Riding, 'Staging The Raft of the Medusa', *Visual Culture in Britain* 5:2 (Winter 2004), pp. 1–26. The article abstract notes that 'in 1820 three separate spectacles on the subject of the shipwreck of the Medusa (1816) were available to the British public. All were based, or claimed to be based, on the narrative of two raft survivors, Henri Savigny and Alexandre Corréard. These "spectacles" were the exhibition of Theodore Géricault's *The Raft of the Medusa*, William Thomas Moncrieff's nautical melodrama *The Shipwreck of the Medusa: Or, The Fatal Raft!*, and Messrs Marshalls' *Grand Marine Peristrephic Panorama of the Shipwreck of the Medusa French Frigate with the Fatal Raft*. While the melodrama and the panorama differed significantly in their interpretation of the events surrounding the original shipwreck they were both connected by the painting through plagiarisms or the performance of tableaux, and thereby engaged, consciously or not, with Géricault's singular interpretation and artistic vision/intentionality.'

4 See Guignery '"History in question(s)"', p. 54.

5 One of the texts consulted by Barnes was Don Cameron Allen, *The Legend of Noah*, Urbana: University of Illinois Press, 1963.

6 One source for Barnes of the James Bartley whale story comes from Gerald L. Wood (ed.), *Guinness Book of Animal Facts and Feats*, Guinness World Records Limited; Second Revised edition, Norwich: Jarrold and Sons, 1976.

7 For this chapter, Barnes drew on Steven Callahan's book *Adrift: Seventy-six Days Lost at Sea*, Boston: Honghton Mifflin, 1986.

6

Tell me yours: *Talking It Over* and *Love, etc*

This is my truth, tell me yours.

Aneurin Bevan

Revisiting some of the themes and dynamics from Barnes's first two novels, *Talking It Over* (1991) and *Love, etc* (2000) are companion pieces centred on the relationships between three characters. Stuart, Gillian, and Oliver are also the principal narrators and take turns to tell aspects of the story from their own point of view. Stuart and Oliver are unlikely school friends who, in a way not entirely dissimilar to Chris and Toni in *Metroland*, have developed a close but uneasy relationship into adulthood. In the first novel Stuart and Gillian marry and the unfolding story follows the loquacious and erudite Oliver's growing obsession with Gillian, who eventually leaves Stuart for his best friend. The sequel throws this process into reverse as the practical and dogmatic Stuart tries to win Gillian back; it concludes with Gillian still married to Oliver, but pregnant by Stuart. Each of the three characters muses over the possible futures they have, with or without each other. An ending that resists closure is made more open by the characters' appeals to the reader to choose: Oliver asks which of his three plans 'you' would prefer; Stuart asks whether 'you' think Gillian could come to love him again; and Gillian asks if 'you' think Stuart still loves her now. A final few lines are delivered by Gillian's French mother Mme Wyatt, who answers noncommitt-ally for the reader: 'Don't ask me anything. Something will happen. Or nothing' (LE, p. 250). Arguably, such an ending underscores Barnes's own resistance to conclusions, certainties, and categorisa-tions that distort the particularities of life and art in the search for grand narratives.

Though ironic with respect to its contents, *Talking It Over's* title highlights its approach. With no narrator between characters and reader, different voices alternately speak as though to an interlocutor or camera, taking into a modern idiom many literary predecessors and archetypal settings, including a component of the primal situation of oral story-telling by the fireside or to listeners seated in a circle. The reader is to be told a story, but it is to be recounted from three sides, with occasional additional 'asides' from others who know the three protagonists. In fact, reading the novel is sometimes akin to witnessing statements from characters at a court hearing where the testimonies have been interspliced and placed occasionally in direct dialogue – the extent to which Gillian, Oliver, and Stuart appear aware of each other's accounts varies in the novels; sometimes they ask the reader what is going on but at other times several characters are seemingly present together (e.g. TO, pp. 218–19). However, the principal pattern of the first book is established as Stuart speaking, then Gillian, and then Oliver. This is the template for the opening chapters and it is not until the seventh chapter that another voice is introduced. The reader appears to be addressed throughout and is, for example, offered a cigarette by Oliver and told by Stuart not to give him 'that look' (TO, p. 160). The form of this address suggests a professional or semi-formal occasion, but it is hard to perceive exactly in what role the reader is placed (Stuart's ex-girlfriend Val calls the implied reader 'the manager' TO, p. 218). It is thus part of the artifice of the novel that it invites the reader to see situations from the point of view of each of these strangers but have no attributed identity within the fiction beyond the 'role of the reader', implied and actual. Stuart offers to shake hands with the reader, literally introducing himself as a character in the first two pages. Questions are also posed to the reader and, for example, in chapter 19 of *Love, etc* answers are given to questions that have been supposedly asked by the reader.

In Barnes's previous novel the enemy of love was history, but a sense of the time of writing, of the contemporary, was almost entirely absent. In *Talking It Over*, Barnes responds directly to the rhetoric of the times, the 1980s and early 1990s. Here, the enemy of love is capitalism, the market, and *homo economicus*. Also, where the previous novel presented a variety of voices sequentially, each one stating their viewpoint, *Talking It Over* mixes them together (there are nine in all but three predominate). In 'Parenthesis', from *History of the World*, where Barnes talks to camera, he warns us that love does not guarantee happiness. Love fails; love often makes people unhappy. This is in part what *Talking It Over* is concerned with; indeed the failure of love to bring happiness could be said to be what the pronoun in the title refers to. Like three people at a marriage guidance session, Gillian, Stuart, and Oliver talk it over, with the actual reader resembling a silent non-directive counsellor, wordless before the statements, answers, entreaties, and questions uttered by the characters and, though never included in the text directly, by the implied reader.

Like each of Barnes's previous novels, *Talking It Over* is in part a comedy. It could also be summarily described as a multi-sided confessional novel, a farcical tragedy, a would-be *ménage à trois* drama (LE, p. 15), a *Jules et Jim* homage (TO, pp. 23–4), and a dysfunctional version of *La Ronde*, where each character in the hermetically sealed erotic circle pursues a different lover. At any point in the novel there is a couple – Oliver and Stuart, Stuart and Gillian, Gillian and Oliver. Thus, adopting a familiar approach in Barnes's work, it appears a variant on his first novel's three-part structure, which had three sequential pairings: Toni and Chris, Chris and Annick, Marion and Chris. That Gillian is half-French and the fourth most important character is her mother, Mme Wyatt, adds to the sense of a resonance across the novels. The tripartite structure also contributes to the sense of truth existing inbetween versions that occurs throughout Barnes's work. 'What I tell you three times is true' (TO, 157) is a line that could summarise the approach to truth in the novel if one understands it to mean that the three versions offered by Oliver, Gillian, and Stuart, contain more than any one of their accounts.[1]

At the start of *Talking It Over*, all three main characters are in their early thirties. Stuart works in a bank, and Oliver works, intermittently, as a language teacher to foreign students. Gillian is a picture restorer, and her quiet care and preservation of art works are enlivened by the occasional exposure of hidden parts of pictures behind the surface paint (she was to have been a social worker in Barnes's earlier thinking, and in the finished novel she trained as one, TO, 56). Stuart is positioned as a materialist, while Oliver sees himself as a romantic: 'the purpose, the function, the bass pedal and principal melody of life is love' (TO, 139). These are identities that the novel at times reinforces but at others interrogates. They unravel in the complexities of characters delineated over five or more hundred pages where the lightness of mood gradually drains from the start of the first book to the final chapters of the second, darker novel. In 'Parenthesis' Barnes concluded: 'The materialist argument attacks love, of course; it attacks everything. Love boils down to pheromones, it says' (HW, 245). Barnes dismisses this approach to love because it would similarly conclude that music played on a violin is reducible to mere bits of wood and gut. The beauty and passion of the playing are not demeaned by the building materials from which the instrument is made; humans and musical instruments are far more complex than their physical materiality: neither Hamlet nor a flute is easily played through knowledge of construction. Yet, in *Talking It Over* and *Love, etc*, there is little consistency in what is being talked about just as there is little basis to the title's promise of communication between Stuart, Gillian, and Oliver: the characters do not talk it over so much as take it in turns to put their case, which is where the book differs from most comparable play performance arrangements or even an epistolary novel, but for the most part resembles a series of interleaved dramatic monologues. The second novel's title was in fact the one Barnes wished for the first book, but it was already in use by another recently published work. Given this fact about the author's wishes, love arguably features less in the two narratives than one would expect. The books are about money, relationships, and sex as much as they are about love. This is to say the 'etc' figures more prominently as competing viewpoints about motivation and priorities circulate in the different characters' discourse. For example, Stuart states that Oliver 'says he only took the job [at the Shakespeare School of English] because the neon sign always cheers him up; but the fact is he really needs the money' (TO, p. 19). Neither reason appears to approach the truth but provides an insight into the priorities to which each character ascribes importance.

Gillian is the least vocal of the three and usually the least engaged with the confessional process: 'Wherever you turn nowadays there are people who insist on spilling out their lives at you . . . Why do they have to talk about it all?' (TO, p. 8) She is also aware that this may marginalise her perspective: 'Just because I don't have a confessional nature doesn't mean that I forget things . . . What I remember is my business' (TO, p. 8). By the end of the first novel, Gillian's is the voice the reader most likely distrusts least. Particularly, as Barnes intended, when she starts to describe the French village

where she and Oliver settle (TO, pp. 240–4). This longish section
starts 'Now listen to me. To *me*' (TO, p. 240), expressing her frustration at the men's dominance of the story; but by the end she has
lost faith in the implied reader's ability to find her engaging: 'You're
not interested in this, are you? Not really. I'm boring you, I can tell.
You want to hear about other things' (TO, p. 244). Gillian's earlier
reluctance to commit to active participation in conversations with the
reader is in part based on a realisation that different parties will mis-
understand, whether it be the other characters or the reader: 'That's
the trouble with talking it over like this. It never seems quite right
to the person being talked about' (TO, p. 39). Similarly 'the trouble
with talking about yourself the way Stuart is doing is that it makes
people jump to conclusions' (TO, p. 38). Gillian sees the talking
exercise, of whatever kind it is, as a game in which Stuart and Oliver
are indulging (TO, p. 39). Her involvement takes time to emerge but
when it does her voice is more persuasive than either of the men's,
perhaps precisely because of the reluctance to divulge complicated
truths and personal details to strangers but also because she fears
stereotyping: 'Every situation is ordinary and every situation is also
unique' (TO, p. 39). This fear is then immediately confirmed by Oliver's
theory that, because her own father absconded with a schoolgirl, Gillian
has been attracted to Stuart as a substitute father-figure. Gillian is
also distrustful of language: 'Words don't always hit the mark do they?'
(TO, p. 58) and speculates as to whether this drew her to the silence
of her work, dedicated to the solitary restoration of paintings. A
metaphor emerges here as Gillian explains her task sometimes to be
one of removing 'overpaint' and revealing something that someone
else had tried to conceal, as when she discovers a boar in a scene of
horsemen, revealing it to be a hunt. The removal of others' additions,
coverings, and over-elaborations appears to be a role she enjoys.
She has found that in many cases it 'completely changed the picture'
(TO, p. 59) to take away some overpaint – her narrative then passes
on to Oliver, the character most associated with 'laying it on thick'
in his monologues. The metaphor also inflects the book's title, suggesting that talking it over is less about talking it through than
covering it over, re-emphasising the narrative's reliance on unreliable
narration. Gillian later explains to Oliver: 'Finding something you
didn't know was there, when you take off overpaint, that's the best.
Watching something two-dimensional gradually turn into something
three-dimensional' (TO, p. 119). Yet, this should not encourage the

reader to believe there is a 'correct version' to be unearthed: 'There is no "real" picture under there waiting to be revealed' (TO, p. 120).

Stuart's principal metaphor in the book is of the cuckoo clock weathermen: joined by a metal bar they are inseparable but only one can enjoy the sunshine (TO, pp. 67–8). This gains resonance as the plot develops for Stuart and Oliver with each character's happiness seemingly predicated on the unhappiness of the other. Oliver's more literal choice of metaphor occurs a little later as he drives Gillian and Stuart home from their honeymoon: 'We're stuck in this car on the motorway, the three of us, and someone (the driver! – me!) has leant an elbow on the button of the central locking system. So the three of us are in here until it's resolved' (TO, p. 80). Oliver adds another person to this triangle by observing that the reader is there too, reinforcing the sense of breaching the fourth wall.

Returning to the start of *Talking It Over*, Gillian's comment that 'what I remember is my business' allows Oliver to launch into a hymn of praise to his memory, peppered with *bons mots* and *aperçus*, while Stuart has already opened the book by proclaiming 'My name is Stuart, and I remember everything' (TO, p. 1). There are two reasons to disbelieve that either man remembers events well. First is the book's epigraph, a Russian saying quoted by the composer Shostakovich in his *Memoirs*: 'He lies like an eye-witness' (TO, p. 220). Second is the treatment of memory across Barnes's work. From *England, England* to *Arthur & George*, memory is positioned as unreliable at best and mendacious at worst. In *Nothing to Be Frightened of* he says: 'My brother distrusts most memories. I do not mistrust them, rather I trust them as workings of the imagination, as containing imaginative as opposed to naturalistic truth' (NF, pp. 244–5). Along similar lines, Barnes also quotes another Russian composer, Stravinsky: ' "I wonder if memory is true, and I know that it cannot be, but that one lives by memory nonetheless and not by truth" ' (NF, p. 228). Thus it is in one way that the 'lies' of eyewitnesses lie strewn throughout the book, but that is perhaps not to say that the lies are intentional, merely that they are memories. The characters have these to go by, while the reader has a tapestry of interwoven monologues based on memory threaded through the narrative. Oliver claims that 'My way with memory is to entrust it only with things it will take some pride in looking after' (TO, p. 10). This is a typically entertaining but enigmatic statement that implies far more than it says. It is both a boast and an excuse rooted in Oliver's innate sense of intellectual

superiority allied to a general tendency towards an amused vanity in
his self-regarding moments: 'my dark, dark hair and kissable ivory
teeth, my slim waist, my panache and my linen suit with the ineradicable stain of pinot noir' (TO, p. 13).

In his notes for the novel, Barnes drew thumbnail sketches for the
three central characterisations:

> Gillian: the force of constant/full adoration is irresistible; love opens
> you up to more love. She marries Stuart because he makes a husband;
> she doesn't say much at first, then later starts talking. Stuart: stolid,
> English, pinstriped in mind, decent, thinks in near-cliches; a Thatcherite
> in the city, but idealistic and uncapitalistic in love. Oliver: Only knows
> what he wants when someone else has it. Falls in love as she comes
> out of the wedding. He's liberal/green/artistic, but in love, Thatcherite.

Barnes also goes on to chart the primary change that each character
is intended to make: 'S changes – disillusionment. G changes –
stronger. O stays the same' and these character trajectories are interesting to chart in the second novel also, where it might be said Stuart
grows stronger, Gillian stays largely the same, and Oliver becomes
depressed.

The first chapter of *Talking It Over* ends with Oliver stating
'Everyone to his own taste' (TO, p. 15). This engages with the title of
the chapter 'His, his or her, their' which foregrounds the grammar
of sexual politics. Oliver's closing remark positions him clearly as
someone who rejects the overthrow of *man*-made language, which
he would certainly argue for in terms of aesthetics and grammar
(cf. TO, pp. 3–4). Stuart has explained that he rejects the pedant's
argument used by Oliver and is in favour of 'their' while Gillian adopts
the compromise position.

At various points, it is assumed in the monologues that the
implied reader disapproves of a character, particularly Oliver: 'You
think I'm a patronising pudendum, don't you?' (TO, p. 27), he says,
and then Stuart pleads a little later 'Please don't take against Oliver
like that' (TO, p. 32). These comments appear to be made in the real
time of the story, suggesting that the characters are not remembering from some future point but that their lives are developing alongside their conversations with the reader. Stuart thus tries to excuse
Oliver at the start of the third chapter in terms he would not employ
later: 'He hasn't got a girlfriend, he's practically penniless, he's stuck
in a job he hates' (TO, p. 32). Chapter Four brings the story into the

present: 'It's now. It's today' (TO, p. 47) says Stuart before asserting two pages later at the start of Chapter Five that, with Gillian's arrival in his life, 'Everything starts here' (TO, p. 49). As Oliver has begun to realise he loves Gillian on the day of her wedding to Stuart, he similarly ends the chapter by asserting that 'Everything begins here' (TO, p. 66) when he meets the couple at the airport on their return from honeymoon. For each of the two men, happiness rests on a future with Gillian but the unacknowledged basis for this possible contentment is a lifelong competitive rivalry.

There is a possible shift between the two books in terms of the characters' communication with the reader and any putative setting for this interaction. *Talking It Over* seems to operate as a series of mini-interviews conducted by an individual, the reader, who interacts with the characters one-to-one. They have some knowledge of what each other is saying, as well as some ignorance (e.g. 'I expect Oliver's given you the impression that I was a virgin when I got married', TO, p. 50). In the seventh chapter, the established sequence of Stuart speaking followed by Gillian and then Oliver is broken and there is also an interview with, or at least testimony from, the young florist Oliver visits six weeks after the wedding to buy flowers for Gillian. Unusually, Michelle has her age placed in brackets, perhaps to situate her comments as those of a late adolescent, and offers the first outside perspective on a character. Her view of Oliver is provided later on the same morning she encounters him, and her verdict is damning: 'if only he hadn't opened his mouth' (TO, p. 89). At this point, the implied *mise en scène* of the novel changes once more, suggesting a series of voices speaking to the reader through the long-established literary conceit of omniscience. The chapters from then on often refer to the present and the impression is of conversations occurring as events happen.

The second novel opens with the impression that Oliver, Gillian, and Stuart are assembled together again, at least at the start. *Love, etc* begins with the three characters wrangling, and Gillian asserting: 'If we're getting into this again, we have to play by the rules. No talking amongst ourselves' (LE, p. 7, echoing Val's comment in the first novel that 'this is against all the rules', TO, p. 218, and Gillian's father's aside, 'I shouldn't be talking to you, I'm sure it's against the rules', TO, p. 235). If we assume this is the situation for the entire book, Gillian, Oliver, and Stuart thus talk about and across each other in sequential monologues that do not constitute a dialogue. However, the most interesting explanation for the format of the novels is provided within them. When Gillian goes to see her mother about the love triangle she now finds herself in, she declares: 'Maman, I thought there were *rules*' (TO, p. 167). She is of course talking about love and marriage, but this is the language in which, as discussed above, the staging of the novel is referred to: in terms of 'rules'. Which is to say that, like matters of the heart, there are no 'rules' that will be observed by all, only market forces, or overpainted stories, or the actions and attitudes of those who think love is the only important thing in life and those who believe in the 'etc.'. Mme Wyatt concludes 'anything that is possible is normal' (TO, p. 168). However, Gillian thinks otherwise: 'There had to be rules. There had to be very firm rules, that's obvious, isn't it? You can't just "be happy"; you have to manage happiness' (TO, p. 253).

The second chapter of *Love, etc* makes it plain what the characters' preoccupations now are. Stuart focuses on betrayal, Oliver on guilt, and only Gillian on love: 'What people want to know, whether they ask it directly or not, is how I fell in love with Stuart and married him, then fell in love with Oliver and married him . . . Being in love makes you liable to fall in love' (LE, pp. 15–16). This echoes the Chamfort-quoting Mme Wyatt's comments in *Talking It Over* when she confesses to the reader that she had an affair only a year after her wedding: 'the beginning of the marriage is the most dangerous time because – how can I say this? – the heart has been made tender' (TO, p. 166). Her confession of an affair is also shadowed by Gillian's revelation that when she met Stuart she was trying to get over an affair with a married man who 'wouldn't leave his wife' (TO, p. 173). These possible parallels and echoes are voiced in the book in several ways but most noticeably by Val, Stuart's ex-girlfriend, who avers that Oliver also tried to steal her from his best friend (TO, p. 186), drawing the conclusion that Oliver actually covets Stuart just as Terri in *Love, etc* will conclude after years of marriage to Stuart that he just wants Gillian.

The title *Love, etc* is explained in the first novel by Oliver's memory of reading letters to *The Times*, his father's paper, that signed off with the expression 'Yours &c'. For Oliver the revised phrase illustrates 'the only division between people that counts' (TO, p. 125): those who believe love is at the *heart* of life with everything else merely an *et cetera*, and those who do not. This is expanded upon later by Stuart when he declares he is 'a materialist' (TO, p. 231). He muses here

on the connections between love and money. First, that the investment of value in money is a collective social fiction, and, second, that
the 'other world illusion, the other thing that exists simply because
everyone agrees to place a certain value on it, is love' (TO, p. 230).
He believes also that, while love is overvalued, money has its consolations; a view he derives from seeing Oliver carrying a copy of
Boethius's *The Consolations of Philosophy*. Money, he argues, is much
more reliable than love as a source of happiness: it provides con-
solatory consumer goods whereas 'love is just a system for getting
someone to call you Darling after sex' (TO, p. 234). In the United
States, where he flees after his break-up with Gillian, he therefore
buys sex and pays to be called 'Darling' afterwards. He now agrees
with Oliver that 'Love operates according to market forces' (TO,
p. 233), which Oliver once used as a metaphor to explain why Gillian
was leaving Stuart for him (TO, pp. 161–2). Stuart now sees two systems in operation in this market. These are 'Pay Now', which he uses,
and 'Pay Later', which 'is called love' (TO, p. 233). Oliver's ill-advised
observation, attempting to use Stuart's language, was, in his own words,
'that human passions operate not according to some gracious rule-
book of courtly behaviour, but following the gusts, the veritable hur-
ricanes of *le marché*' (TO, p. 159). While reflecting different concerns
prevalent in the late 1990s, such as the health benefits of proper nutri-
tion and organic produce, in *Love, etc* the comparisons from the 1980s
between love and the market continue: Stuart names his first business *Le Bon Marché* and hires his future wife to run the front-of-house
operation in one restaurant, while Gillian reads of pre-nuptial agree-
ments for the first time: 'this suggestion in the papers that marriage
should be treated as a business' (LE, p. 37). The enemy of love is no
longer history, but the dominant forces left in the aftermath of the
end of history in 1989: capitalism and consumerism.

    While family life is not much present in the first novel, mothers
and fathers play significant roles in the narrative. Mme Wyatt, Mme
Rives, who is a surrogate mother-figure for Stuart, and Mrs Dyer, who
is a surrogate mother for Oliver, appear as a chorus of well-meaning
older characters commenting from the side. Mme Wyatt enters
the narrative (TO, p. 143) like a relationship counsellor when her
daughter's marriage is in crisis. Her view is that of the wise parent
who can put the situation in a wider context of affairs and marital
breakdowns: 'I have no opinion of such a situation in general, I only
think that such things happen' (TO, p. 144). While in *Love, etc* she

herself is pragmatic about how she is perceived ('I am considered wise by some people, and that is because I hide my pessimism from them', LE, p. 39), others both acknowledge and question Mme Wyatt's status as sage. Stuart in the first novel labels her as 'my wife's snooty mother' (TO, p. 191), though he comes to correspond with her later and to be pleased she is having an affair (TO, p. 250). Gillian explains how she sees her mother in a different light in *Love, etc* (LE, pp. 82–3), largely on the basis of a perception of how Mme Wyatt charms others, including the reader. A short scene with Mme Wyatt, described by Gillian, suggests that she, like Stuart and like Oliver, has a habit of placing difficult choices before Gillian. This happens on the eve of her second wedding when Mme Wyatt realises Gillian proposes, at Oliver's request, wearing the same suit she wore when she married Stuart. Appalled, Mme Wyatt leaves her daughter on her own and later returns from Gillian's flat with two alternatives. Gillian says 'you choose' to her mother but is told she must decide herself. Gillian then makes a strange comparison: 'It's like saying, Look, Gill, I'm afraid you can't marry Oliver tomorrow, that's out, so who would you like to marry instead? This one or that one?' (TO, p. 198). Barnes presents this pattern throughout the novel, of Gillian being asked to make choices at the desire of others. It is only at the end of *Talking It Over* that her agency comes to the fore. While Stuart goes into hiding in France and Oliver seems less colourful without the contrast of Stuart as a foil (TO, p. 256) Gillian chooses to have a child with Oliver (he is all for 'trundling along') and arranges, via an elaborate charade, to effect Stuart's departures from their lives.

Though absent, fathers also impact on the behaviour of Gillian and Oliver. Gillian's father left Mme Wyatt after 15 years of marriage and is a marginal figure, though he has a small speaking part. Oliver's father is also reported to be a major negative influence on his son from childhood, though Stuart is sceptical: 'his father used to beat him when he was a small boy. What with? A rolled-up sweet paper?' (TO, p. 163). Stuart returns to the theme later, expanding on the story by saying that it began at the time Oliver's mother died, when he was about six (TO, p. 171). Stuart merely believes the story 'is a great sympathy-winner, not least with women' (TO, p. 171), and this reminds the reader of the earlier scene where Oliver explains to Gillian that 'My father used to beat me up, you know' (TO, p. 149). Oliver goes on to say that because he reminded him of Oliver's dead

mother his father would hit him with a billiard cue on the legs, until
one day after many years Oliver stood up to him (TO, p. 149). Gillian
notes about the scene that 'Oliver's probably got less self-confidence
than Stuart' (TO, p. 148) but Oliver's confession, provided while trying to persuade Gillian to leave Stuart for him, keenly anticipates
Stuart's suspicions, whereas Gillian's judgement is reversed at the
start of *Love, etc* when she states that Oliver always had more self-
confidence than Stuart (LE, p. 3). Oliver's father dies in *Love, etc* and
his story of childhood beatings is repeated with some further gloss,
such as Oliver's 'zeal' for arson (LE, p. 28), which leaves the reader
in considerable doubt about what to believe. 'The law of unintended
effect' is a phrase of Stuart's that Oliver riffs on in *Love, etc* (LE,
pp. 72–3, p. 81) and uses to explain how life feels to have
operated for Gillian, Stuart, and himself. It is a view countered by
Mme Wyatt's viewpoint that there is not much solidity to Oliver, and
his emotional collapse after the death of his father prompts her to
comment on an 'ineradicable' characteristic of the human race: 'to
be surprised by unsurprising things' (LE, p. 89). Mme Wyatt is not
surprised by Oliver's breakdown, because close familial feelings are
complex; Stuart's explanation is simpler: that Oliver is a liar and his
father was not the bully he claimed (LE, p. 113).

The books' concern with memory is also reignited at the start of
the second novel. While *Talking It Over* began with a discussion over
what and how much each character remembered, *Love, etc* commences
with Stuart surprised that the implied reader does not remember him,
with Oliver sure the reader remembers Oliver, and Gillian unsure. The
opening of the first volume thus concerns itself with the characters'
ability to remember while the second, ten years later, commences with
a question over the reader's. Oliver still does not distrust his memory, but sees it in terms of imaginative energy – 'Our memories
are just another artifice', he asserts (LE, p. 13) – and only for the
benefit of the reader will he unravel a conventional narrative that
purports to be about truth: 'I'll pretend that memory is laid out like
a newspaper' (LE, p. 18).

In *Love, etc* Gillian and Oliver have two daughters. While Gillian
is a success back in London, Oliver takes to screenwriting but ends
the novel mired in clinical depression. For his part, while in the United
States Stuart ceases to work in a bank after two years and establishes
a restaurant before eventually setting himself up in organic food

distribution. He weds an American woman, Terri, and their marriage lasts five years. This second novel is more thematically arranged than the first, and chapters sometimes run through a series of pro-nouncements, riffs, or expatiations on a theme. Chapter Fourteen, for example, provides synopses of each character's view on love, sketch-ing a shorthand description of their current understanding: Stuart states that 'First love is the only love'; Oliver that 'As much love as possible is the only love'; Gillian that 'True love is the only love' (LE, p. 171). 'Love is my life and it is my liberty,' Oliver pronounces, yet the evidence of love in his life is rather slender. Gillian loves her children and, still looking for rules for living, makes her marriage with Oliver work. Stuart believes love is never the same for different people and it is something about the self that is learned; he there-fore says that he has learned that he will only ever love Gillian, never anyone else (LE, pp. 158–72), and this is a belief corroborated by the testimony of Terri.

Having all the last words in the chapter, Stuart also concludes that love does not lead to happiness, does not make someone a better person, and does not make an individual liable to fall in love as much as not being in love does. Stuart's deeply pragmatic attitude towards love leads to his bullish destruction of Gillian and Oliver's marriage, with assertive and sometimes aggressive displays of putative kind-ness from giving Oliver a job, through reinstating them in the home he once shared with Gillian, to forcing himself on Gillian, who becomes pregnant. The novel moves towards a dark conclusion as Stuart is positioned as the engineer of the plot by Oliver, mani-pulating the reader as much as he does anyone (LE, p. 239). Elli, Gillian's assistant who has been romantically matched with Stuart, says she feels more conned by Gillian (LE, p. 240). To Gillian the key question is whether Stuart still loves her, and for Stuart it is whether she can love him again. Continuity, cycles, and reversibility are repeated touchstones in the novels, which often move entertainingly along predictable lines set in motion by the characters' pursuit of love, while the realisation that the pursuit of love will not make them happy dawns gradually for each.

For the reader, a key question is whether there is more to come, turning the companion pieces into parts of a triptych. To complete the triadic form of the overall story, it is quite possible Barnes will write a third volume about Stuart, Gillian and Oliver, which will presumably continue to operate on the principles of *plus ça change plus c'est la même chose,* and *plus c'est la même chose plus ça change*: 'Reversibility – lustrous watchword of my wife's profession' says Oliver (TO, p. 205).

Note

1　This is a quotation from Lewis Carroll's 1874 poem *The Hunting of the Snark*.

7

We won't get fooled again:
The Porcupine

Much of this would be intolerable without a sense of irony.
Julian Barnes, 'Candles for the living'[1]

The Porcupine (1992) appeared first in Bulgarian (translated by Dimitrina Kondevo as *Bodlivo Svince*) and was only later in the same year released in its original English. It is the political fable of liberalism's lack of conviction before ideological certainty, set in an East European country moving from communism to liberal democracy, and is informed far more by Bulgarian history than by that of any other country. Its human story centres on the overthrown Party leader Stoyo Petkanov, who is brought to trial for prosecution by the ambitious and aggrieved Peter Solinsky. Barnes has said of the book:

> When I wrote *The Porcupine*, I deliberately used a traditional narrative because I felt that any sort of tricksiness would distract from the story I was trying to tell. A novel only really begins for a writer when he finds the form to match the story.[2]

In formal terms, *The Porcupine* indeed appears to be a traditional narrative and seems almost pointedly to confound critics' expectations. It is political, realist, and, though not without ironical passages, serious; yet it also displays the characteristics of Barnes's other works. That is to say it remains sceptical of idealism and refuses either to see events from one side or to take comfort from political or religious rhetoric. The sense persists of an uncommitted, slightly detached, and therefore seemingly well-balanced authorial presence: one that detects disturbing traces of sound reason and logic in the justifications offered by Petkanov and sees Solinsky as someone with power and history, rather than morality, on his side. Barnes is in no wise a simple reactionary but is predisposed to see the arguments on both

sides, and put them to the reader, asking like Gillian and Stuart in
Love, etc.: 'what do you think?'

Barnes became interested by Bulgarian politics on a book tour and
enlisted the support of local people to help him research and situate
the novella. In brief, Bulgaria was a Balkan country of about eight
and a half million people under control of the USSR at the end of
the 1980s. Elections took place in June 1990 when the Communist
Party gave up its power following the breakdown of the Soviet bloc
the previous year. The Bulgarian Socialist Party (BSP) won these first
Assembly elections, though with only a small majority, but was
brought down by a general strike in late 1990 and replaced by a
transitional coalition government. The Union of Democratic Forces
(UDF) formed a government and later also held the presidency
when President Zhelev was elected for a five-year term in Bulgaria's
first popular presidential vote in 1992. His victory ended communist
hopes of clinging to power though the margin of victory was relatively
narrow in both cases, reflecting the persistent appeal of communist-
inspired policies. Zhelev was appointed president in August 1990 and,
in a country previously largely dependent on trade between the communist bloc countries, many blamed him for the economic shocks since
the collapse of communism. With foreign debt totalling £6 billion,
unemployment approached 25 per cent and inflation exceeded 30 per
cent. Nearly all property remained under state ownership but Zhelev
announced there was no alternative to privatisation and a market
economy. Bulgaria had been previously dominated for decades by
Todor Zhivkov, who was put on trial in 1991.[3]

Yet, the story Barnes tells is not an isolated one but a representative
parable about the opposition between strong and weak ideologies
at the level of personal conviction and national history. Other East
European communist leaders were also toppled at the same time as
Zhivkov: Honecker, the East German leader, resigned in October 1989
and was taken to Moscow by the Soviet army. Gustav Husak ran
Czechoslovakia for 20 years until the velvet revolution in 1989. He
was reviled for supporting the 1968 invasion and died in 1991.[4]

Barnes's idea for the novella was 'to have a moral trial' of the old
order, epitomised by the ex-leader. There is a tension throughout
between different opinions over the purpose of the trial: does it
represent a desire for a reckoning of the past or is it a show trial?
The book's title is never explained beyond Solinsky's reference to
treating Petkanov with 'porcupine gloves', an allusion to a question

about holding someone with 'porcupine-gloves' in Pushkin's (1799–1837) 'The daughter of the commandant' (1836) – the phrase is thought in the story to come from a Russian proverb and its meaning is debated but seems to imply 'show him no liberty'. Barnes's title appears to be a reference to the prickly and dangerous Stoyo Petkanov for most of the novella but by the end of the narrative it arguably refers more accurately to his courtroom usurper, not least because 'porcupine-gloves' are gloves made of porcupine-skin, not gloves for handling porcupines. The tyranny of conviction politicians may have been overthrown but the plasticity of careerist politicians has arrived.

The novella's timescale appears to be roughly from the end of 1990 to spring 1991, and its narrative follows three parallel stories. First is that of Petkanov, the Dictator. The sections here consider his incarceration, the opening of his trial, and his encounters with the prosecutor Peter Solinsky, ending with Petkanov not being seen to be guilty enough. Second is the examination of Solinsky, which includes the background of his father's story, difficulties with his wife Maria's family, and his temptation to secure a conviction on fabricated evidence. Last there is the counterpoint of the lives of a group of students, whose viewpoint illuminates the wider perspectives of the people.

More generally, the novella puts the deposition and trial of a former Eastern bloc Communist dictator into a wider context of historical transition and political compromise. Though *The Porcupine* was written soon after the events it chronicles, there is no recourse to snap judgements about the fall of communism or the triumph of democracy. Barnes instead situates the moment as one turning-point in a long road of historical change that turns back on itself more than it progresses. The perspectives represented in the book are manifold, but two figures sit at the centre of national and media scrutiny. On the one hand the hard-line ex-leader, full of confidence and rhetorical power, on the other the newly appointed ambitious liberal-intellectual prosecutor, tasked with denouncing the dictator but without much of a case in terms of evidence. A kind of staged trial is to be waged for the nation to purge its anger and its recent past, to achieve the renewal that is alluded to in one of the book's endings when prosecutor Solinsky places two *martenistas* (woollen tassels) under a stone – tradition and peasant wisdom dictates the meaning of what will be found there two days later: 'Any living thing that stirred promised you fertility, a new beginning' (P, p. 129).

Petkanov is on trial for 'Mass murder. Genocide. Ruining the country' (P, p. 32). However, he argues he should really be charged with 'bringing peace and prosperity and international respect to this country' (P, p. 121). Petkanov's attitude to his trial is that he is being condemned for his commitment to the socialist cause that history has for the moment overtaken. 'I was the helmsman of this nation for thirty-three years, I was a Communist, I sacrificed my whole life for the people, therefore I must be a criminal according to those who once made the same promises and swore the same oaths that they now betray' (P, p. 126). Petkanov concludes he is a scapegoat for the country's denial of its own character after its anti-communist *volte face*. Petkanov positions himself in the trial as a man who will always stick to his principles rather than change his stripes to suit the new times that Gorbachev's reforms have instigated. In this trial of worldviews and world systems, he thus takes the moral high ground as the one person who is true to his beliefs while others, he maintains, are hypocrites: once they claimed loyalty to the old system and now they claim allegiance to the new. His prosecutor, Peter Solinsky, is one of those he would cast in this light, and his motives for becoming Petkanov's prosecutor include personal ones: 'Peter Solinsky had grown up within the Party. A Red Pioneer, a Young Socialist, and then a full party member, he had received his card shortly before his father fell victim to one of Petkanov's routine purges and was exiled to the country' (P, p. 25). The cost of the public trial for Solinsky is the loss of his personal life: 'my father is dead, my wife wants a divorce and my daughter is refusing to speak to me' (P, p. 135). His wife is suspicious of his motives for applying to be prosecutor general, calling him a 'TV lawyer' (P, p. 127), and then appalled that he tries to introduce the charge against Petkanov of murdering his own daughter. 'It's a show trial, Peter' she says in her final words to him, and her charge is justified by the explanation Solinsky has given her earlier for suddenly introducing new evidence: 'If Petkanov hadn't signed that memorandum, he must have signed something like it . . . the document is true even if it is a forgery. Even if it isn't true, it is necessary' (P, p. 113).

As mentioned above, Barnes's novella effectively works with three narrative strands: that which follows Solinsky, that which follows Petkanov, and that which follows the four students who watch the televising of the trial in order to witness history being made. A third-person narrator reports events and describes the thoughts and actions

of the people involved in these strands, which are woven around the
political story-line of the old system's dismantling.

When Petkanov is 'packed off by the Central Committee to his house
in the north-east province with a five-man guard for his own protection'
(P, p. 21), his deputy Marinov ineffectively tries to take control, then
the Communist Party suspends its own rule, proposes a coalition,
and subsequently calls for elections. The other parties oppose this,
because they have had no time to prepare and the Communist Party
owns the media, but they are given no choice. The Socialist (formerly
Communist) Party wins a narrow majority and asks the opposition
parties to work with it. They refuse and the country descends into
political wrangling, inadequate reforms, and black market trading. The
women's protests that start the novella are a reaction to this state of
affairs: there is no work but much corruption and high inflation The
final part of this phase of post-Eastern bloc realignment is the trial
of Petkanov: the 'end of the beginning' (P, p. 22).

Dark and light imagery operates throughout the novella. The book
starts with the city 'abnormally dark' while Petkanov is lit inside his
room by the 'low wattage of the desk lamp' (P, p. 1). The women's
procession outside is lit by 'thin, yellow candles' as weapons of
protest. In the Cathedral square, until recently a forbidden area, 'the
darkness was concentrated' with only one street lamp in six giving
out 'its exhausted glow'. The women conserve and pass on their lights:
'To save every match but the first, each new candle was lit from the
flame of another' (P, pp. 1–2). The women are protesting against
the Party and the lack of food in the shops. At the story's conclusion,
the Cathedral is now alight: 'Candles blazed at him, the polished brass
was fiery, and small high windows focused the sun into thin hard
rays'. The candle-stand is a 'theatre of light' and Peter Solinsky's eyes
adjust 'to a brightness that depended upon surrounding darkness'
(P, p. 137). This triumph of candlelight and of private faith represented
by a resurgence of churchgoing is, however, not the last light mentioned in the novella.

This appears in the final scene of an 'old woman', contrasting
with but echoing the story's opening words about Petkanov 'the old
man'. She clutches a framed portrait of Lenin outside the vacant
Mausoleum of the First Leader and holds a vigil in the rain with only
'thin light veering off the wet glass' in contrast to the 'flashing brief
light' of locomotives illuminating the fallen statues of communist
leaders dumped on waste ground (P, p. 138). The woman represents

an obstinate and continuing faith in communism, despite the abuse and heckling of passers-by: 'whatever the words, she stood her ground, and she remained silent' (P, p. 138). Also, her resolution mirrors the spirit of Petkanov who for the length of the book stands alone against the tide of feeling rushing against him. She also represents the difference in viewpoints across generations, and the reader takes her to be Stefan's grandmother, first encountered going out on what by the end of the book we understand to be this lonely vigil, with her woollen scarf and hat and the picture of Lenin from her wall (P, p. 54). She appreciates a longer perspective on political history than her grandson or his friends can imagine: 'How long would it be before the Party was banned again, forced to go underground? ... Ahead she saw an inevitable return to the oppression of the working class, to unemployment and inflation being used as political weapons' (P, pp. 54–5). She expects a future revolution to continue the cycle in opposition to those who would see the moment as marking an end of history and the triumph of capitalism, as proposed by Francis Fukuyama in his 1992 book *The End of History and the Last Man* which foresaw the triumph of Western liberal democracy following the collapse of the Soviet bloc, eventually leading to an age of equality and universal enfranchisement that would be characterised by the political correctness of mutual recognition and respect but also a potentially disastrous flattening of human experience.[5]

With regard to the novella's ending, Barnes explained in a letter the significance of the final paragraph, noting that it is in triadic form and picks up on the opening section, though instead of thousands of women there is one protestor and she is without candlelight (as is Lenin) but echoes a wider expectation from many of those who take the long view of a return of the old system. In the meantime, the new world Stefan's grandmother fears is evident in the behaviour of his generation. They spend much of their time watching TV, glued to the media trial, and denounce Petkanov unremittingly in spite of and irrespective of any arguments he makes. Their interest is not in the case against him, but in revenge and humiliation marking 'the Changes', as events are called, avoiding the term and taint of 'revolution'. The new generation is shown not only to be in many ways shallow and self-regarding but capable of being vindictive and spiteful. Vera is upset that men no longer look at her in the street (P, pp. 52–3) while her male friends are disrespectful (calling Lenin 'granny's boyfriend' to Stefan's grandmother's face, P, p. 54), mindlessly abusive (P, p. 120), and supportive of anti-democratic processes – arguing that there should have been no trial because this was a story with only one side to it (P, p. 71). The four of them wish to witness history, seeing the trial naively as marking the beginning of true justice and complete honesty: 'It was the end of lies and illusions; now the time had arrived when truth was possible, when maturity began. How could they be absent from that?' (P, p. 20). Their youthful idealism, which sees only a change in history, is contrasted with the older people's awareness of cycles and patterns. This is also present in the figure of Alyosha, the 'heroic bronze soldier, left foot advancing, head fixed nobly high' (P, p. 8). At the close of the book, this 'Statue of Eternal Gratitude to the Liberating Red Army' (P, p. 8) has been taken down in a further cleansing gesture designed to expunge the nation's past, a psychological necessity like the demonizing of Petkanov: 'On a low hill to the north of the city stood a concrete pedestal, sullen and aimless. The bronze panels round its sides gleamed dully in the damp. Without Alyosha to lead them into the future, the machine gunners now found themselves fighting a different battle: irrelevant, local, silent' (P, p. 138). The removal of the statue is a culmination of a debate staged earlier in the novel, in which the counterargument was put forward that such a removal would be expensive and in any case 'You did not destroy the Pyramids in retrospective guilt at the sufferings of the Egyptian slaves' (P, p. 44). Here as elsewhere the narrator is entirely non-committal, reporting the views of different citizens but expressing none, as though sceptical of all standpoints, and yet the implied loss of innocence and integrity is clear through the earlier characterisation of Peter Solinsky's patriotic and communist fervour inspired by Alyosha (P, pp. 8–9).

There are several interesting political micronarratives encoded in the book. One works with the aphoristic commonplace that a political society can be judged according to how women are treated. While *The Porcupine* ends with an old woman and an old man (Petkanov is presented this way at the start of the novella) both looking towards a return to communism in the future as the only socialist defence against Western corruption and capitalist decadence, there are great differences between them, even if the students see Petkanov as Stefan grandmother's 'sweetheart' (P, p. 132). One is a privileged dictator who believes that women should be confined to the home. He also argues that the state of the Western world can be judged by the way Reagan and Gorbachev are dominated by their wives, whom he believes they cannot 'control'. He also believes this of Peter Solinsky. By contrast Stefan's grandmother is a weak old lady abused by a younger generation, fearful of the rise of pornography around her, and starkly alone in contrast to the demonstrating women at the story's opening. She might represent the stoicism of the people, and the final words of the novel, ironically, describe both her obstinacy and her lack of a voice: 'she stood her ground, and she remained silent' (P, p. 138).

As with much in the novella this can be read in several ways; an observation pointed up by a subplot, that of the Devinsky Commando. This student group is named after a poet who 'had a reputation as an ironist and provocateur' (P, p. 45). All their slogans and chants are subversive, from the insincere proclamation on their banner 'We, loyal students, workers and peasants, support the government' to a simple insubordinate kiss given to a soldier, which results in the officer's rapid promotion through the ranks (P, pp. 46–9). The Commandos' final act is to send Solinsky an anonymous postcard saying 'Give us convictions not justice!' (P, p. 127). This echoes the concluding remarks made by Petkanov at the trial: 'Everyone, every-one in this court and who is a witness to this show, knows that the charges against me are convenient inventions' (P, p. 126). This is aimed at Petkanov's 'former comrades' but particularly at Peter, who was once a loyal party supporter but who has pragmatically and perhaps opportunistically turned against his former beliefs. This defection was initially to the Green Party, where he still has connections:

> Perhaps he should get a new place to live, as Maria had suggested. He could mention it to the Deputy Minister of Housing, who like him had been an early member of the Green Party. Just because Maria wasn't coming with him, it didn't mean he had to live in a dingy mouse-hole. Six rooms, perhaps? A prosecutor general sometimes has to receive foreign dignitaries at home. (P, p. 128)

Building on an earlier decision not to accept the offer of a larger apartment because it would be unwise to accept any 'visible sign' of government favours during the trial (P, p. 114), this piece of ration-alisation occurs as Peter Solinsky looks out at numerous housing blocks, including the one in which he and Maria used to live: 'a small apartment in the Friendship complex (block 307, staircase 2)' (P, p. 7). Peter has in part given into a self-serving pragmatism that has been most evident in his preparedness not to convict Petkanov

with real evidence: 'The document is true, even if it is a forgery. Even
if it isn't true, it is necessary. Each excuse was weaker, yet also more
brutal' (P, p. 113). Ironically, until presented with forged evidence by
Security Chief Ganin, the best Peter can do is accuse Petkanov of using
his influence to give an actor a larger apartment (P, p. 59).

Here we can see a continuing concern with truth and self-deception
in Barnes's fiction. This kind of logic is evident in the arguments used
by Stuart and Oliver in *Talking It Over* and *Love, etc.* Lovers and politicians are similarly unreliable it would seem, in that each wishes for
something to be true even if it isn't. To not do this is courage in
Barnes's fiction, epitomised in his fourth novel by Jean Serjeant's
willingness to stare life and death in the face. Barnes's novels are
littered with self-deceivers from Graham Hendrick in *Before She
Met Me* to Arthur Conan Doyle in *Arthur & George*. His fiction is also
littered with those who make compromises with life but do so
through acceptance rather than wilfulness, from Chris in *Metroland*
to Martha in *England, England*, the book we shall examine next. As
this book has tried to argue throughout, Barnes is a comic novelist
and it would be short-sighted to see *The Porcupine* as largely devoid
of humour when it is akin to a satire of the kind more explicitly
undertaken by Ian McEwan in the Booker-prize-winning *Amsterdam*
(1998) on the British sleaze society cultivated by the Conservative
government in the late 1980s and early 1990s. This is evident in the
constant use of misunderstandings, hyperbole, litotes, caricature,
detachment, and so on, to achieve ironic effects in a story of for-
geries, subterfuges, lies, intrigues, and deceptions. It is arguable also
that the blank narrator is in fact a deadpan one, the only kind that
its story deserves. Barnes has played no tricks but he has presented
an ironical story in which everyone is either a victim or is deluded
or corrupt or mistaken.

The Porcupine is arguably a warning from history more than any
kind of committed political novel. The third-person narrator is non-
committal and characterless but the narration juxtaposes scenes and
characters to create repeated ironic effects. The book's standpoint
appears to be that times of political change breed simple judgements
and invoke a monochromatic rhetoric in which individuals are
branded good or evil and political expectations are pitched in dan-
gerously unrealistic terms that appeal to the heightened feelings of
the situation. Peter Solinsky's sense of contamination by the end of
the story illustrates this as he has lost both his life and his integrity

to the trial. He has used deception and forgery instead of admissible evidence to, it seems, do a right thing in entirely a wrong way, because he thinks Petkanov needed to be found guilty to purge the conscience of a nation and slake its thirst for vengeance: 'welcome to the modern world' Solinsky concludes (P, p. 129). If this is Barnes's view of politics encoded in fiction it suggests a deep distrust of the machinery of power, which corrupts almost all whom it touches in this novella no matter what the political system.

Barnes also portrays the passion of Petkanov along the lines of fanaticism, and explores the staunch political stands of others, from Thatcher to Khomeini, in his collection of correspondence from 1990 to 1995 for the *The New Yorker*, *Letters from London*. Solinsky is the less compelling character because less dramatic and more human, in terms of his frailties and failings as well as his desire for justice. The advantage of the triumph of democracy initially appears to be a new freedom of speech to express dissatisfaction with the economic situation and to articulate the general public's indifference: 'permit me to inform you that I don't give a fuck either way' (P, p. 128). Barnes's scepticism of large political schemes and national projects is also evident in his next novel, *England, England*, but here the contrast is not between communism and capitalism but between the two extremes of an imagined community of the nation, pitting pre-industrial bucolic island against 'postmodern' heritage theme-park isle.

Notes

1 Julian Barnes, 'Candles for the living', *London Review of Books* 12:22 (1990), pp. 6–7, p. 7.
2 Interview with Guppy, 'Julian Barnes: the art of fiction CLXV', pp. 73–4.
3 Zhivkov might have been put on trial for the poisoned umbrella assassination of Georgi Markov in London. Cf. pp. 91–5 of *The Porcupine*.
4 For a detailed analysis of the relationship between Barnes's fiction and the historical record see Vanessa Guignery, 'Untangling the intertwined threads of fiction and reality in The Porcupine by Julian Barnes' in Vanessa Guignery and François Gallix (eds), *Pre and Post-publication Itineraries of the Contemporary Novel in English*, Paris: Editions Publibook Université, 2007, pp. 49–72.
5 Francis Fukuyama, *The End of History and the Last Man*, London: Hamish Hamilton, 1992.

8

History doesn't relate: *England, England*

> What Robin Hood was or who he was, in the dim underwoods of history, is unimportant. It is what folk history has made him that matters.
>
> *John Fowles*[1]

Like the appeal in his short story 'Melon' to think of 'England, England and the future' (CC, p. 81), Barnes's extended fiction of that name is a novel of ideas of the nation over time. It is a fictional study *around* issues such as the creation of the past, the re-fashioning of an imagined national community, and in particular the telling and selling of England.[2] It is a self-reflexive novel concerned with postmodernism in terms of its content, though perhaps not its form, which is broadly conventional. The novel is laden with irony but it has a sinister streak that suggests, certainly if we think of *The Porcupine* as a post-Soviet *Animal Farm*, that *England, England* is in part a descendant of Orwell's *Nineteen Eighty-Four*.[3] Barnes's narrative dwells on the betrayal or at least reinvention of language and authentic experience through a rewriting of the national past. This is compared to an individual recasting of memories over time, where the inaccurately remembered rather than actual past shapes the subject's conscious sense of identity.

England, England explores the relationships, *inter alia*, between heritage and commercialism, history and exploitation, imitation and reality. It is a fantasy, but one that has many recent echoes and real-life parallels. Its central story is that of a powerful businessman who plans to turn the Isle of Wight into a colossal theme park so that tourists will not have to traipse from Dover to London to Stratford-on-Avon to Chester. Asked about his choice of location, Barnes said in interview with the *Daily Telegraph* that the Isle of Wight was one of the first places in Great Britain to be perverted by becoming a tourist destination. It was a rather undeveloped, old-fashioned, quite primitive offshore island until sunbathing became fashionable. Queen Victoria and Tennyson went there and that did for it. Sea-bathing became all the rage. The traditional industries of smuggling and boat-building lost out to tourism.[4]

In Barnes's novel, the Isle of Wight imports all the main cultural-commercial aspects of the mainland, which is itself transformed into 'Anglia', a technologically backward nation which gradually regresses into its own past, becoming a rural country dominated by spurious folk myth and pagan ceremonies. Barnes has said of his novel 'it's about the idea of England, authenticity and the search for truth, the invention of tradition, and the way in which we forget our own history'.[5]

England, England is also a novel around rather than about the simulacra of memory, identity and self-construction. The narrative opens with Martha Cochrane asserting that she has never come across a first memory that is not a lie. This is because the answers people give are not their first memories but the misremembered, re-remembered latest imagining they bring to mind when asked the question. A first memory is more lost than knowledge of birth, about which some facts at least are likely to be known. Barnes's interest in this question is not confined to *England, England*, however. Oliver, in *Love, etc*, when asked by his doctor to give recollections of his child-hood, replies that he cannot remember 'how many are truly mine and how many purloined from the Cyclopedia of False Memory' (LE, pp. 199–200). *Arthur & George* also opens with a discussion of first memories: George Edalji 'does not have a first memory, and by the time anyone suggests that it might be normal to have one, it is too late. He has no recollection obviously preceding all others' (AG, p. 3). Arthur Conan Doyle believes he does have a first memory, of something he saw: his grandmother's corpse. Yet, the narrator asks pointedly about the first time, sixty years later, that Arthur speaks of the incident in public: 'How many internal retellings had smoothed and adjusted the plain words he finally used?' (AG, p. 3). This is a point revisited across Barnes's writing, culminating in his comment in *Nothing to Be Frightened of*: 'We talk about our memories, but should perhaps talk more about our forgettings' (NF, p. 38). In *Arthur & George*, Barnes proceeds to write alternately the early memories of the two boys, emphasising that fiction-making is a way to find the truth that memories cannot, for all their supposed veracity and actual falsifying through layers of revision and selective recollection. Memories are not true for Barnes, but they are constitutive of identity and he opens *Arthur & George* by suggesting it is 'the acquisition of memory' that perhaps makes us most human (AG, p. 3).

Martha's false first memory involves a jigsaw puzzle of the counties of England, personified as an old lady sitting on a beach: 'and you know what children are like with jigsaws, they just pick up any old piece and try to force it into a hole' (EE, p. 4). This becomes not just a metaphor for the forcing of memory but a metonym for Part Two of the book, in which pieces of England are assembled and forced into place to provide a potted toytown version of the country. Exploring the false memory of England lies at the core of Barnes's novel: 'the past was never just the past, it was what made the present able to live with itself' (EE, p. 6). Barnes compares personal memory and national history in terms of self-deception because an 'element of propaganda' always intervenes between external and internal perceptions (EE, p. 6). Barnes puts forward the example of popular perceptions of Francis Drake: gentleman hero to the English, pirate to the Spanish. This is a subject ranged over in Barnes's fiction on other occasions. For example, in 'Evermore' from *Cross Channel*, another of his female protagonists wonders 'if there was such a thing as collective memory, something more than the sum of individual memories. If so, was it merely coterminous, yet in some way richer; or did it last longer? She wondered if those too young to have original knowledge could be given memory, could have it grafted on?' (CC, p. 100).

Martha also has 'lucid and significant memories' she mistrusts, such as the day of the Agricultural Show, which stands for the bucolic way of life still imagined to be at the heart of the true England after centuries of industrialisation. Martha has kept the schedule of prizes from the Show, and its list presages the inventory of the fifty quintessences of Englishness that appears later in the book. School is then remembered as religious chants – assembly – followed by history learnt by rote from the Roman Invasion in 55 BC to the Treaty of Rome in AD 1973. The teacher 'led them in and out of two millennia, making history not a dogged progress but a series of vivid and competing moments' (EE, p. 12). Similarly, character formation is expected to be something up to the individual – 'you build your own character' – whereas Martha finds she is shaped by her experiences and spots of memory, such as her father leaving the family and taking a miss-ing piece of 'her England' with him, leaving only an oak leaf behind. As the years go by, Martha's self-image is eroded and she disposes of the jigsaw puzzle of England; she becomes uncomfortable and unsure about the story of her personal and national identity: 'She did not know whether she was meant to remember or to forget the past. At this rate she would never build her character' (EE, p. 17). Yet, time constructs it for her and she finds she is building her future mem-ories and making her own mistakes, thus escaping the desire to blame her parents, which develops as her creed: 'after the age of twenty-five, you were not allowed to blame anything on your parents' (EE, p. 22).[6] When her father does reappear, however, she blames him for some-thing: for not remembering that she used to do jigsaw puzzles, and that when he left the family he walked off with Nottinghamshire in his pocket.[7]

The incident is echoed by the next novel we will examine, in *Arthur & George*'s similar interest in a place at the 'beating heart of the Empire' (EE, p. 17). For the Edaljis this is Staffordshire at the seat of national identity in the 'centre of England, yes, where we find ourselves' (AG, p. 42). Both Arthur and George have become English: 'Irish by ancestry, Scottish by birth, instructed in the faith of Rome by Dutch Jesuits, Arthur became English. English history inspired him; English freedoms made him proud; English cricket made him patriotic . . . for Arthur the root of Englishness lay in the long-gone, long-remembered, long-invented world of chivalry' (AG, p. 23); George similarly 'is English, he is a student of the laws of England, and one day, God willing, he will marry according to the rites and ceremonies of the Church of England. This is what his parents have taught him from the begin-ning' (AG, p. 42). Education, experience, and memory together school the individual in self-fashioning, which at the level of the country is presented simply as a collective 'heritage'.

Part One of Barnes's novel is entitled simply 'England'. The second Part of the novel is called 'England, England' and implies that England at the turn of the millennium is defined not by the Church, the law, culture, geography, or even history but by 'heritage'. It con-cerns Jack Pitman's pocketing of all the country, to be reassembled on the Isle of Wight like pieces of a jigsaw puzzle. He is bringing together the most-remembered parts of the stories of England's past, as though drawing up an itinerary for a tourist package-tour. Barnes has said in interview:

The tycoon was based to some extent on Robert Maxwell, the press baron, who was a grotesque rogue. *England, England* is my idea-of-England novel . . . England as a functioning country is comparatively rich and healthy; many elements of society are comparatively happy. That may be the state of England; but, whether it is or not, what is the idea of England? What has become of it? The English are not very self-conscious the way the French are, so I wanted to consider the idea of England as the millennium turned. England as an idea has become somewhat degraded, and I was interested in what happens if you pushed that, fiction-ally, to an extreme. You take some of the tendencies that are implicit in contemporary Britain, like the complete dominance of the free mar-ket, the tendency of the country to sell itself and parody itself for the consumption of others, the increasing dependence on tourist dollars; then you add in one of my favourite historical notions, the invention of tradition.[8]

Linking *England, England* to Barnes's previous novel, another political fiction concerned with the state of the nation, is the figure of the media mogul Robert Maxwell whom Barnes mentions here.[9] When working on *The Porcupine*, Barnes had been surprised by the answer given to his question of who will help Bulgaria post-communism: 'Robert Maxwell says he will help them, which is a dismaying thought. To be introduced to the delights of capitalism by Robert Maxwell? By Robert Maxwell, friend and publisher of Todor Zhivkov? Not sur-prisingly, Bulgarians are wary of the Great Benefactor, though his name is much in evidence.'[10] Barnes also outlined his thoughts on Maxwell in his essay 'Fake!', which uses as its title a word he con-spicuously left out of *England, England*:

> The only other tycoon of similar standing to have been so stigmatised in the last quarter of a century was the newspaper magnate (and pub-lisher of Ceausescu, Zhivkov, Husák, and Kádár) Robert Maxwell, who was described in 1971 by a Department of Trade and Industry inquiry as being 'not in our opinion a person who can be relied upon to exer-cise proper stewardship of a publicly quoted company'. Needless to say, Mr Maxwell has continued to run an increasing number of publicly quoted companies. (LL, p. 30)

Pitman is thus part-modelled on the figure of Maxwell, who, it emerged after his death in 1991, had used hundreds of millions of pounds from pension funds to save his companies from bankruptcy.[11] Barnes was thus interested to use a figure noted for the fraudulent manipulation of people's lives and livelihoods as the head of a fake project of historical identity reformation.

The French intellectual brought in to theorise Sir Jack's project declares that it is thoroughly modern because it aims at that which is old: 'We in our country have our certain idea of *le patrimoine*, and you in your country have a certain idea of 'Eritage' (EE, p. 53). Though this Baudrillardian character wishes to distance Pitman's project from this quaint idea, the rise of heritage culture is central to the invention of tradition that Barnes is satirising. As one character says, 'the point of *our* history . . . will be to make our guests, those buying what is for the moment referred to as Quality Leisure, *feel better*' (EE, p. 70). Under the names of preservation and conservation, heritage culture thus seems to domesticate the radical past as a consumer product. Barnes's French intellectual argues that we aren't happy with the genuine old because it threatens us with an alternative reality to our own; 'the replica is the one we can possess, colonise, reorder' (EE, p. 55). 'All that was once directly lived' quotes the Intellectual 'has become mere representation', and this lies at the hub of the preference for heritage over history (EE, p. 54).[12]

Novels that critique heritage culture are as common as those that exploit it, but, in cultural terms, literature often offers the templates for heritage nostalgia, especially on film. The expression 'heritage cinema' has gained currency since the critic Andrew Higson first essayed a description of historical costume drama and literary adaptations that followed in the wake of the television adaptation of *Brideshead Revisited* (dir. Charles Sturridge, 1981), which epitomises some of the quintessences of Englishness in Barnes's novel, such as numbers 27 (TV Classic Serials) and 28 (Oxford/Cambridge) (EE, pp. 83–5). Arguably, the first film to critique the heritage genre presciently appeared at the same time and starred one of the same actors, Jeremy Irons, in a screen version scripted by Harold Pinter of a novel that signalled a turn in literary historiography, *The French Lieutenant's Woman* (dir. Karel Reisz, 1981). Like the novel it adapted, the TV series of *Brideshead* is a model of heritage sentiment because it shows, and to an extent shares, nostalgia as well as depicting its object: from the TV production's perspective of the last quarter of the twentieth century, Charles Ryder dreamily reminisces towards the close of the Second World War about a golden past into which the viewer is guided, as into a museum, by a Proustian voice-over extolling the beauty of times *not lost* but (re-)shown. At the centre of this, the Marchmain family are recollected in Ryder's embellishments, providing one influential template for heritage commentary in a long, gilded analepsis. As Evelyn Waugh wrote in the preface to his revised version of *Brideshead Revisited* in 1959, 'the book is infused with a kind of gluttony, for food and wine, for the splendours of the recent past, and for rhetorical and ornamental language which now, with a full stomach, I find distasteful'. Such cultural ostentation promotes a different kind of country living from the Agricultural Show of Martha's childhood: it is a cherished bygone age of country-house aristocracy and high culture, but one which none the less packages the past as a consumer product accessible to all as part of the collective heritage.

The contemporary appropriation of the word 'heritage' that Barnes is dealing with came to the fore in the 1980s to describe a drive towards requisitioning the past in the cause of national pride across both culture and politics. As Higson points out, this new meaning differs from the dictionary definition in which heritage is deemed to be 'received or inherited'.[13] 'Heritage' culture is not that which is handed down from the past to the present, as illustrated by *England, England*, but that which is superimposed on to the past by a present generation, and Higson notes, for example, that 'heritage cinema' both lingers on interior opulence or landscaped exterior shots and privileges the culture of the upper and middle classes over that of the working class, which is also generally true of the classic novel used for adaptations.

Fuelling debates over the pros and cons of conservation, National Heritage acts in 1980 and 1983 gave an official political context to the work of archivists, film-makers, and also novelists interested in not just preserving or restoring aspects and images of the past but reorienting the (re)production and consumption of them. English Heritage was established by the 1983 act to maintain nationally important buildings and monuments while the Heritage Educational Trust was set up in 1982 to encourage the exploitation of their social and educational value. Subsequently, film was the most obvious medium in which the new heritage movement reached cultural prominence, but it did so through the adaptation of significant narratives from British history and classic fiction, especially Austen, the Brontës, James, Forster, and Hardy. The director–producer team exemplifying heritage film, (Ismail) Merchant and (James) Ivory adapted in quick succession Forster's *A Room with a View* (1986), *Maurice* (1987), and *Howards End* (1992), followed by a modern counterpart in Ishiguro's *The Remains of the Day* (1993).[14] Most such adaptations conform to an orthodoxy exhibiting rose-tinted nostalgia for a bygone class-bound imperial England, paralleling a Conservative government agenda that advocated the embrace of anachronistic values and a reverse of the radical social changes associated with the 1960s and 1970s. Heritage cinema productions, such as *Elizabeth* (1998), the film released in the same year as *England, England* about the reign of the first Queen,[15] for the most part commodify the past without acknowledging, or reflecting upon, its repackaging, thus echoing Victorian and other reinventions of the national past to interpellate citizens as imperial subjects, for example. By contrast a dimension of self-reflexive awareness on this point of critical acknowledgement characterises contemporary novels such as *England, England*, though Barnes overtly implies that historical truth is almost unachievable, whereas other contemporary British writers like Barry Unsworth and Penelope Lively incorporate that awareness into their fictions.

In his analysis of those films that share some of these infusions, like Barnes's English quintessences informing the island-story of his Wightwash, Higson focuses on conservative elements that had all appeared in cinema before but started featuring more regularly and in combination: the Elizabethan and Victorian eras, the country house, rural landscapes, the upper classes, nostalgic selectivity, classic novels or glossy recreations of key moments in national history. His most salient point notes the shift in temporal understanding of 'heritage' to denote that which is reconstructed of the past, though Higson fails to foreground less reactionary political aspects, from feminist to democratic modes of representation.[16]

As suggested by Barnes in his novel, current literary critiques of heritage nostalgia crucially take place in a different mode from fabrications of the past because of the context of late capitalism in mass consumer society. While Shakespeare's history plays, using a four-hundred-year-old example, rewrote history with real personages for partly propagandisitic purposes, replicated in versions like Laurence Olivier's patriotic film of *Henry V* in the Second World War, there is now a trend towards critiquing the advertisers' approach that reinscribes the past to suit current taste for the purposes of marketing more than national revisioning (Olivier's *Henry V* is a nationalistic film, Branagh's 1989 version a heritage one). In Ian McEwan's screenplay for Richard Eyre's film *The Ploughman's Lunch* (1983), the supposedly ancient but in fact recently invented pub meal of the title indicates how a manufactured past such as Jack Pitman's can be profitably sold as authentic, just as the film's protagonist is rewriting the Suez crisis to meet the expectations of current Anglo-US relations in the context of the Falklands War. While this revisioning is apparent in national policy, the national curriculum, the media, and heritage cinema, it applies less clearly to literary fiction where a more self-conscious approach has dominated. Because of the novel's capacity for introspection this can be taken to an extreme in the satire of *England, England* and similar national comedies. Barnes's novels had, for example, two counterparts published in 2005, both illustrating how contemporary historical fiction often insinuates a double-consciousness by foregrounding present understanding and past re-presentation: a reality-show state-of-the-nation version in James Hawes's *Speak for England* and a personality-based fantasy in Rupert Thomson's *Divided Kingdom*, where the UK is broken into quarters to house different British personality types: the sanguine, choleric, melancholic, and phlegmatic.

In *England, England*, the French intellectual's quintessentially British term 'heritage' has other, problematic associations which need noting in order to illustrate the reflective element that distinguishes the strain of recent fictional critiques exemplified in Barnes's novel. Towards the end of the 1980s, the critic Robert Hewison put forward the contention that 'we are manufacturing *heritage*, a commodity which nobody seems able to define, but which everybody is eager to sell, in particular those cultural institutions that can no longer rely on government funds as they did in the past . . . At best, the heritage industry only draws a screen between ourselves and our true past.'[17] While announcing a problematic belief in the notion of a true past, Hewison thus partly sees the rise of 'heritage' investment as an economic response to the removal of grants and subsidies under the Thatcher governments of the 1980s. As the arts and humanities, like other areas, are required to pay their way in the marketplace the most saleable 'products' often appear to be appealing versions of the past that combine history with mythopoeic tropes, constructing narratives that aim less at accuracy than accessibility, in Hewison's sense of the experience of 'living in a museum'. This is not sufficient reason to subscribe to a monologic notion of the 'true' past. But it is reason to distinguish an impulse to re-create the radical alterity of history from an attempt to provide an entertainment experience for cultural tourists in a media age that commonly sees the past in terms of an exploitable foreign country, as Jack Pitman does. This is to recognise that in Britain, since the end of Empire, history has to a degree displaced geography in the sense of providing fertile ground for a ready appropriation of difference that remains politically acceptable in a glob-alised world.

For Hewison, heritage culture replaces a critical sensibility in which he says, referring to writers such as Barnes, 'even the radical wing of postmodernism betrays a deep, if parodic, obsession with the past'[18] In heritage consumer capitalism, where critique is fragment-ary, and in an accelerated culture where the contemporary can be redundant in the time it takes to write and publish a novel, the pre-sent seems often to be neglected for the escapism of nostalgia. The History Matters campaign launched in 2006 began with the perspective 'History is not the story of strangers, aliens from another realm; it is the story of us had we been born a little earlier'.[19] The social critic Patrick Wright queried this standpoint, whose aims were laudable, precisely because it familiarises the past in order to make us more comfortable with its strangenesses. The danger attendant on this is a tendency to allow people too easily to insert themselves unchanged into the past, as in Michael Crichton's Hollywood film *Westworld* (1973) where four historical 'worlds' (the American Frontier West, Ancient Rome, a Robin-Hood *lite* medieval England, and Futureworld) are avail-able to holidaying customers, in full costume dress.

The attempt at truthful representation in art remains for most novelists in some sense a necessary aim despite its impossibility, and this is something Barnes moves on to in *Arthur & George*. Fiction by its very definition has no such necessary compulsion as historio-graphy to be verifiable. Neil McEwan notes that recognition and respect for 'the primacy of evidence' is fundamental for historians,[20] whereas for many novelists 'how to be true' to a past from the parallax view of the present remains a methodological issue, if not always a seri-ous concern. For Barnes in most of his writings, the way to be true is to eschew pretensions towards truth: to draw attention to artifice, metaphor, ludic narration, and the ineluctable potential of writing to deceive in its forlorn attempt to en-textualise the world.

In terms of the contemporary novel, narratives that engage with the turn to 'heritage' that *England, England* critiques, such as *Arthur & George*, can arguably be distinguished within historical fiction by their use of notable real persons or signal historical moments but most importantly by the element of double-consciousness. Many contemporary British writers of historical fiction eschew techniques which try to recreate the past faithfully, as would be the aim of a novelist such as Mary Renault for example, but to engage from the perspective of the present with the discourses and literary styles of the period, purposefully using, in the example of Fowles's *The French Lieutenant's Woman*, 'a convention universally accepted at the time of my story: that the novelist stands next to God'.[21] In its reversion to the past much of the most discussed historical fiction now offers a revision, often juxtaposing documented historical viewpoints and present perspectives implicitly (as in *Arthur & George*) or insinuating a hierarchy of discourse through direct commentary (*The French Lieutenant's Woman*) or staging a dramatised 'romance of the archive' with parallel past and present narratives (A. S. Byatt's *Possession*).

However, *contra* writers like Barnes, there are those who have defended heritage culture, such as the British historian Raphael Samuel, who notes that 'Aesthetically, as well as historically, heritage is a hybrid, reflecting or taking part in, style wars, and registering changes in public taste'.[22] He argues that today 'the past is seen not as a prelude to the present but as an alternative to it, "another country", and "heritage" is more typically defined as relics under threat'.[23] Samuel argues that the dominant intellectual position on 'heritage' is that it tries to 'commodify the past and turn it into tourist kitsch',[24] to which he responds by maintaining that it has been both popularly and commercially successful, responding to an interest in public history and stimulating curiosity in the past. Samuel observes that, along with traces of simple anti-pastoralism, social condescension, and misogyny in the critical response, '[l]iterary snobbery also comes into play: the belief that only books are serious . . . Artefacts – whether they appear as images on the television screen, in costume drama, or as "living history" displays in the museums and the theme parks – are not only inferior to the written word but, being by their nature concerned with surface appearance only, irredeemably shallow.'[25] He rationalises this bias in terms of the historian's familiarity with the library over the museum, with solitary contemplation rather than shared experience, and books rather than crowds as companions. Scholarly routine appears antithetical to attempts at 'living history' that express the past as spectacle and turn away from education towards entertainment, but these are the Jack-Pitman-like activities that mobilise thousands of people, inspire festivals, raise sponsorship, involve collectors, secure government subsidies and win Heritage Lottery Fund money. Samuel concludes: 'Is not the historical monograph, after its fashion, as much a packaging of the past as costume drama?'[26]

Hewison says that postmodernism and heritage are linked because they both 'conspire to create a shallow screen that intervenes between our present lives, and our history. We are given no understanding of history in depth, but instead are offered a contemporary creation, more costume drama and re-enactment than critical discourse. We are, as Fredric Jameson writes, "condemned to seek History by way of our own pop images and simulacra of that history, which itself remains for ever out of reach." '[27] This is more arguably true of the eclectic yoking together of iconic historical pastiches in the presentation of shopping malls than it is of much contemporary fiction, which retains the element of critique that Hewison believes the heritage industry lacks, though he sees it in independent creative artists and writers like Barnes, who can 'alter our perceptions of the material world and release its potential',[28] even when engaging with history, establishing a past using familiar themes of recognition before overturning them, while the heritage industry aims at preservation and veneration instead. His argument is echoed by Patrick Wright, who sees a regressive and reactionary nostalgia in a 'Brideshead complex' counteracting the egalitarian impetus of the welfare state, with the country house as a symbol of everything threatened by modernisation. Heritage is thus seen as a political project aimed at installing a sense of historical identity to replace the discredited notion of imperial destiny in a decayed and declining culture.[29]

In Part Two of *England, England* Martha is the Appointed Cynic to Jack Pitman's project. She is neither sycophant nor opponent: her job is to subvert all statements about the project and to pose alternative questions. Sir Jack employs her to be the internal voice of radical scepticism and disillusionment: someone disappointed by the world so long ago that they have naturalised doubt and forgotten hope. At one point, Martha asks the project's 'Ideas Catcher' and her lover, Paul, about the end to a story he tells about a Russian composer. 'History doesn't relate', Paul replies, thus lacking the point to his own story and unwittingly exposing the parameters of Sir Jack's project, which both deals in the fragmented, (mis)remembered popular inheritance of national education and stands back from engaging with less marketable aspects of the past. 'The point is that most people don't want what you and your colleagues think of as history – the sort you get in books', explains the project's Concept Developer to its Official Historian (EE, p. 70). As I noted above, Martha has earlier thought about this in relation to her own childhood memories:

'It was like a country remembering its history: the past was never just the past, it was what made the present able to live with itself' (EE, p. 6).

Barnes records in his notes kept with the manuscripts for the novel Martha's realisation that the 'search for authenticity is the search for your "nature", which you locate in childhood; hence people's normal obsession with their childhoods (photos etc)'. The novel ponders the question of whether this 'nature' is no more authentic than the 'nature' Sir Jack describes when he walks the countryside and sees from a hill a pheasant by a river beyond a field and a copse: 'The hill was an Iron Age burial mound, the undulating field a vestige of Saxon agriculture, the copse was a copse only because a thousand other trees had been cut down, the river was a canal and the pheasant had been hand-reared by a gamekeeper' (EE, p. 60). Barnes thus points up the postmodernist view that there is no 'original' available in any case: that what we look back to as 'authentic' is often replica: Palladian architecture, Athenian democracy, and so on. What Sir Jack suggests however is that instead of seeing this as loss it should be viewed as refinement or improvement of an original idea.

On 26 January 1997, Barnes wrote a letter to his publishers, Jonathan Cape, about his scheme for *England, England*. In it he explained the plan for the novel:

> Three parts: One and Three both short, about 25 pages, middle section about 200. time-scale c.1980/c2010/c2040 – not that the dating's especially important. It's not a futuristic novel. It's a novel about England, more specifically the idea of England, now, as the millennium turns; it is satirical/playful, especially in the middle section, which is the story of a Project by one Sir Jack Pitman, Maxwellish tycoon and visionary bastard, who constructs a vast leisure centre on the Isle of Wight. It starts from the premise that since tourists have a problem getting from one five-star site to the next, and since (as surveys show) they aren't picky about seeing a replica rather than an original, the best way to help them 'do' England is to gather a version of it together on one site. All the top expressions of Englishness – from Buck House to Stonehenge, the White Cliffs, Manchester United FC, Robin Hood, and so on – are gathered together for ease of visiting. Gradually, it becomes clear that much more is at stake: from a sort of user-friendly, top-dollar heritage centre, the Island begins to rival 'Old England', then supersede it, then offer itself as a sort of model society of the future. The project is monstrous, risky, ridiculous and vastly successful. Running through this satirically-treated structure is the personal life

(to which the whole of Parts One and Three are devoted as well) of Martha Cochrane, clever, half-damaged child, then disillusioned woman, who works for the Project as a Special Advisor and Appointed Cynic. Her story is treated innerly, realistically, as a quiet core running through the noisy main plot. To put it (very) crudely, her story is about the search for authenticity and truth – to yourself, to your nature, to love – taking place amid all the fabulation, replication and commercial clatter of the Project . . . 'Anglia' . . . is what 'Old' England has become by c2040, a by-passed, de-urbanised semi-failure of a place, forgotten beside the success of England, England, which is what the Isle of Wight renames itself.

Inevitably when the Project comes to resemble history, and the actors in 'England, England' start to behave like their real-life counterparts, the island's 'top-dollar' guests are appalled to find that Robin Hood hunts the island's animals and Dr Johnson insults tourists.

Part Two of the novel ends with Martha critiquing Sir Jack's project and shrugging off much of her cynicism, even if a return to innocence is impossible for her. She wishes instead for a return to seriousness, which Dr Max labels 'sentimental yearning': 'No, it's not sentimental. On the contrary, I'm saying life is more serious, and better, and bearable, even if its context is arbitrary and cruel, even if its laws are false and unjust' (EE, p. 237). Martha comes to at least wish to slough off her arch bitterness and put her faith in the solemnity of custom and ceremony based on a belief in original culture, however naive, rather than the postmodern play of 'England, England'. This signals her return to the past, along with the novel's.

In the third Part of *England, England*, the English mainland becomes a parochial backwater. It is depicted as a rural, arcane, ostracised, recidivist country without influence from outside its borders. The Celtic edges of England have been reclaimed by Wales and Scotland, and 'England, England' has taken over all the famous aspects of Old England. Towards the middle of the twenty-first century, Martha returns after many years of travel to this village-based country now called 'Anglia', the title of Part Three. The questions that persist now concern the battles between competing narratives that vie over tradition, the establishment of historical authority, and the vagaries of both life and memory. Part Three enters into dialogue with Part Two through such comments as a schoolmaster's chide that 'folklore, and especially invented folklore, should not be the subject of monetary exchange or barter' (EE, p. 244). The schoolmaster also believes in collective tradition and that established, especially written down, 'myths and legends' are to be welcomed and passed on, but ones that are known to be made up in the present are unacceptable. Martha herself, because she grew up in the country unlike many of the inhabitants of Anglia, is sought out for her memories and authenticity (EE, p. 246), despite the fact that these are the aspects of her life she has most questioned.

Her journey has been mirrored in that of her country, whose jigsaw history has now been reassembled with reshaped pieces in a different order in another place: 'The world began to forget that "England" had ever meant anything except England, England, a false memory which the Island worked to reinforce; while those who remained in Anglia began to forget about the world beyond' (EE, p. 253). Anglia returns to its supposed past, losing its contacts with the outer world and losing its technological prosperity, but reclaiming a seriousness about its misremembered traditions. This concludes in a village Fête to echo the Agricultural Show of Part One. At the Show the seriousness that Martha wished for is clear in the debates over 'real' people, which are no less questionable than the decisions of England, England, but rooted in an innocence and belief that contrasts utterly with the cynicism Martha put to use in Part Two:

> an *ad hoc* meeting of the parish council was called to discuss the question of whether or not Edna Halley was a real person. Jez Harris counterclaimed by challenging the real existence of Snow White and Robin Hood. Some said you were only real if someone had seen you; some that you were only real if you were in a book; some that you were real if enough people believed in you. (EE, p. 264)

Martha remains outside of the village conga line that weaves through the final pages of the book, her inability to regain lost innocence placing her apart from the revellers. The ending recalls two earlier discussions with Dr Max. In the first he explains that he thinks 'England, England' is manipulative, vulgar, and staggeringly commercial, but not bogus, because that word implies 'an authenticity which is being betrayed . . . [I]s not the very notion of the authentic somehow, in its own way, bogus?' (EE, p. 131) This, in addition to Dr Max's other adjectives, leaves a division between the cynical and the serious separating England, England from Anglia. The second discussion recalled by the ending of the novel follows shortly after the first, when Dr Max decides:

R-eality is r-ather like a r-abbit, if you'll forgive the aphorism. The great public – our distant, happily distant paymasters – want reality to be like a pet bunny. They want it to lollop along and thump its foot picturesquely in its home-made hutch and eat lettuce out of their hand. If you gave them the real thing, something wild that bit, and, if you'll pardon me, shat, they wouldn't know what to do with it. Except strangle it and cook it. (EE, p. 133)

In testament to this image, *England, England* ends with Martha hearing a rustle in Anglia: 'Again, not a badger but a rabbit, fearless and quietly confident of its territory' (EE, p. 266). Anglia's history is wild rather than domesticated and Barnes seems to place a virtue in this, while acknowledging that both are based on false memory.

In conclusion, it is noticeable that for all its invention and comedy *England, England* is a book with little plot and few strongly drawn characters, despite its promising beginning. There is much to entertain and amuse the reader but less to engage, and in this the novel imitates its protagonist, Martha Cochrane, whose largely underdeveloped story in the novel's First Part is one of hope and disappointment, innocence and disillusion. This partly explains why she becomes a distant adult in Part Two of the novel: 'You withhold yourself. My observation, and this is in the context, Miss Cochrane, of being fond of you, is that either you participate actively, but in a stylized way, portraying yourself as a woman without illusions, which is a way of not participating, or you are provokingly silent, encouraging others to make fools of themselves' (EE, p. 134). By putting Martha in the background much of the time while the England, England project enters into full swing in Part Two, the novel also withholds some of Barnes's usual strengths and too often adopts a stylised stance towards its material, insufficiently involving the reader. Parts One and Three of the novel are more engaging than the depthless blank parody of Part Two, which perhaps illustrates its own argument too well. The caricature of Sir Jack does not reach beyond what the novel itself sees as the psychological cliché of a powerful man whose sexual thrills rest on self-infantilisation. *England, England* is an entertaining read full of comic brio but the intentionally debased language and crude stereotypes of Part Two make it more of a curio than a tour de force. Happily it did not signal a decline in Barnes's powers as his subsequent, darker, less slapstick writings have been as sharp and insightful as any of his successes from the previous millennium.

Notes

1 John Fowles, 'On being English but not British' in *Wormholes*, London: Jonathan Cape, 1998, pp. 77–88, p. 83.

2 I am alluding here to Benedict Anderson's *Imagined Communities: Reflections on the Origin and Spread of Nationalism*, London, Verso, 1991, which maintains that the spread of Protestantism and print capitalism lies at the core of nation-formation in Europe, overcoming allegiance to Rome and to Latin, or other local languages, creating a sense of commonality among vast groups of people who will for the most part never meet each other but who will have shared and connected narratives of collective identity.

3 Barnes also invokes an Orwellian *Animal Farm* flavour to his comic dystopian vision in *England, England*. At one point, Martha and Paul sit in a wine lodge which sports a 'print of two dogs behaving like humans; around them, men in dark suits yelped and barked' (EE, p. 63). Barnes here plays on the familiar imagery of country pubs, with their tapestries of snooker-playing dogs, to insinuate something more sinister along the lines of *Animal Farm*. It is not just that this is an unnatural state of affairs but that it is a naturalised one.

4 John Lancaster, 'A vision of England', *Daily Telegraph*, 29 August 1998, p. 5.

5 Unsigned, 'He's turned towards Python. (But not the dead Flaubert's Parrot sketch . . .)', *Observer Review* (London), 30 August 1998, p. 15 (interview upon the publication of *England, England*), reprinted in Guignery and Roberts, *Conversations with Julian Barnes*, p. 27.

6 This is a view repeated by Barnes himself in the second essay of *The Pedant in the Kitchen*.

7 Martha's concern with her father is echoed in the diptych of *Talking It Over* and *Love, etc.* in Oliver's deeply conflicted relationship with his father. His father's death precipitates Oliver's emotional breakdown and Mme Wyatt comments on how without parents 'You are supposed to be adult now, grown up. You are at last free. You are responsible for yourself' (LE, p. 91).

8 Guppy, 'The art of fiction CLXV: an interview with Julian Barnes', p. 74. *The Invention of Tradition* is the title of a book edited by Eric Hobsbawm and Terence Ranger, first published by the Cambridge University Press in 1983.

9 The media's dominance of Part Two is flagged by each section starting with a phrase in capitals, imitating the convention of newspaper articles.

10 Barnes, 'Candles for the living', p. 7.

11 Maxwell was not his birth name. He was born with the name Ján Ludvík Hoch into a Jewish family in Eastern Europe. Growing up in a small town in Carpathian Ruthenia, a province of pre-Second World War

Czechoslovakia, he arrived in Britain as a refugee in 1940 at the age of 17.

12 This is Barnes's translation from the opening page of Guy Debord, *La Société du spectacle*, Paris: Éditions Buchet-Chastel, 1967.

13 Andrew Higson, *English Heritage, English Cinema: Costume Drama Since 1980*, Oxford: Oxford University Press, 2003, p. 50.

14 To this can be added Hugh Hudson's *Chariots of Fire* (1981), whose enormous success was one of the catalysts for the genre, Charles Sturridge's films of Forster's *Where Angels Fear to Tread* (1991) and Waugh's *A Handful of Dust* (1987), and even the adaptations of Woolf in Marleen Gorris's *Mrs Dalloway* (1997) and Sally Potter's *Orlando* (1992).

15 *Elizabeth* (1998) and *Elizabeth: The Golden Age* (2007), both directed by Shekhar Kapur, bookended the 2005 mini-series *Elizabeth I*, starring Helen Mirren and Jeremy Irons.

16 Higson also does not historicise his critique in the way that Raphael Samuel endeavours to in *Theatres of Memory. Volume 1: Past and Present in Contemporary Culture*, New Edition, London: Verso, where the 1960s are considered the founding decade (e.g. *The Forsyte Saga* (1967)) for a heritage industry that surfaced on television in the 1970s (e.g. *Elizabeth R* and *Upstairs, Downstairs*) before flourishing in historical costume and films in the 1980s and beyond.

17 Robert Hewison, *The Heritage Industry: Britain in a Climate of Decline*, London: Methuen, 1987, pp. 9–10.

18 Ibid., p. 11.

19 Stephen Fry, quoted in Vron Ware, *Who Cares About Britishness? A Global View of the National Identity Debate*, London: Arcadia, 2007, p. 101. For details of the History Matters campaign see www.nationaltrust.org.uk/main/w-trust/w-thecharity/w-policy-history_matters_update.htm (accessed 23 November 2009).

20 Neil McEwan, *Perspective in British Historical Fiction Today*, Basingstoke: Macmillan, 1987, p. 18.

21 John Fowles, *The French Lieutenant's Woman* [1969], London: Triad/Granada, 1977, p. 85.

22 Samuel, *Theatres of Memory*, p. 211.

23 Ibid., p. 221.

24 Ibid., p. 259.

25 Ibid., p. 267.

26 Ibid., p. 271.

27 Fredric Jameson, *Postmodernism Or, The Cultural Logic of Late Capitalism*, London: Verso, 1991, p. 135.

28 Hewison (1987) *The Heritage Industry*, p. 145.

29 See Patrick Wright, *A Journey Through Ruins: The Last Days of London*, London: Paladin, 1992.

9

Retrospectively imagined memorials: *Cross Channel* and *The Lemon Table*

> He was gone beyond memory, and no plump little French cake dipped in tea would release those distant truths.
>
> CC, 206

Barnes has written two volumes of loosely connected short stories.[1] The first, *Cross Channel* (1995), is explicitly focused on a topic often associated with Barnes and his writing, the relationship between England and France. The second, *The Lemon Table* (2004), engages a number of themes that striate Barnes's work, such as ageing and death. It is a collection that treats in fictional form issues raised by his later memoir *Nothing to Be Frightened of.*

Cross Channel assembles stories of the British and Irish in France across modern history. Its closing story 'Tunnel' concludes by explaining that all the stories have been written by an 'elderly Englishman' who has returned from France on the Eurotunnel train in 2015. This writer stands as a surrogate for the older Barnes, an author who has apparently taken elements of his train journey as imaginative platforms on which to develop the earlier stories. Thus the writer encounters modern-day marauding football-fan 'Dragons' (the title of the seventh story) and sees from the train a First World War cemetery in France that prompts him to think of the inscriptions of names on Lutyens's Somme memorial arch at Thiepval, reminding the reader of 'Evermore'. It transpires that a woman in the compartment is a Master of Wine, which recalls the story 'Hermitage', about two British women who take over a French vineyard, but also the end of 'Experiment', which mentions a female Master of Wine who seemingly provides the key to the narrator's supposition about his Uncle Freddy's Parisian tale of sex and the surrealists. Passing reference is additionally made to both cycling and cricket, the subjects of other stories.

Underlining this connection between the final story and the writing of the others is the theme of memory. This is of course one of Barnes's principal touchstones throughout his writing: as Oliver rather tricksily says in *Talking It Over*, 'If you remember your past too well you start blaming your present for it. Look what they did to me, that's what caused me to be like this, it's not my fault' (TO, p. 15). In certain respects, a similar charge might be made for and against the heritage culture of *England, England*, but it is the twists of memory that figure most prominently in Barnes's writings. He explains, for example, why he thinks that present circumstances affect how we remember the past: 'It's as if some adjusting mechanism is going on all the time which you're unaware of, which is fitting your past and adjusting it to some version of how you've turned out, which you weren't even aware needed a propaganda department to justify.'[2] In 'Experiment', one explanation for this is at least implied: 'when I rebuked my uncle for the contradictoriness of his memories, he gave a contented little smile. "Marvellous, the subconscious, isn't it?" he replied. "So inventive"' (CC, p. 46).

Suspicious as ever of the reconstructive workings of the mind, Barnes in 'Tunnel' uses the phrase 'retrospectively imagined' (CC, p. 197) instead of 'remembered' to exemplify its Wordsworthian attention to the 'tunnel of memory' (CC, p. 210). Barnes is thus interested in connecting the stories across history as imagined reconstructions that have little pretension to 'truth' but, as always with Barnes, do have claims to revealing truths. Such a perspective is personified in the ageing writer: 'This was what he had become: an old man lumpy and misshapen with memories. Except for a fault in the metaphor: memories, unlike vegetables, had a quality of cancerous growth. Each year your string-bag bulged the more, grew ever heavier, and pulled you lop-sided' (CC, p. 210). The conceit of the story collection is underlined here: 'What was he finally but a gatherer and sifter of memories: his memories, history's memories?' (CC, p. 210). This is the case not simply with the relationship the writer has with the preceding narratives, but with the stories' own thematic interest in retrospective imagination. For example, 'His story didn't always begin in the same way' is the opening line of 'Experiment', one of the more unusual stories in *Cross Channel* (CC, p. 45). The line could encapsulate Barnes's approach to questions of history, and also memory.

In 'Melon', Barnes's cricket story, the General admits that he has trouble recalling the names of all the players in his team: 'Normally he remembered Wood. It was Etheridge whom he forgot. Etheridge or Edmeads. Once he had forgotten himself. He had the other ten names but could not seize the eleventh. How could this happen, that a man forgets himself?' (CC, p. 86). This final question rings throughout Barnes's work in which people are repeatedly unsure or distrustful of their memories of themselves. If memory forges identity, forgetfulness feeds imagination but detaches the individual from life; losing the past precipitates an inclination towards death.

In 'Evermore', Miss Moss queries the concept of a 'collective memory' and wonders about the ambiguity inherent in the notion of the passing on of memories. She conjectures whether the young could have memory grafted on to guarantee the inscriptions that confidently say soldiers will be remembered 'For all future time' (CC, p. 100). As in all his writing, Barnes avoids sentimentality here but the story's poignancy rests on the knowledge that all specificity will be forgotten, and the living memory of the war will perish in a general feeling of unease without detail: 'The war would be levelled to a couple of museums, a set of demonstration trenches, and a few names, shorthand for pointless sacrifice' (CC, p. 110). The thematic play with memorials and memory also invokes the trauma of shell-shock, which is embodied in Miss Moss's memories of her short marriage to the shrapnel-wounded Denis: 'he could never remember what had been happening. He had guilt and pain, but no specific memory of what he felt guilty about' (CC, p. 101).

'Evermore' is as much about death as it is about memory, and *Cross Channel* begins with a perspective that looks forward to termination. 'Interference' is a story about an English composer in France that starts with the sentence 'He longed for death' (CC, p. 3). This interest in the individual's emotional relationship with life's endpoint illustrates the main theme of the second volume, *The Lemon Table*, which assembles stories first published between 1996 and 2003. While 'Evermore' conjectures whether 'man is only a clerical error corrected by death' (CC, p. 98), *The Lemon Table* demonstrates that Barnes wishes to focus in his later work on two understandings of 'the end of life'. The first is the death of youth, the second the death of old age (NF, p. 42). When he was himself only approaching a pensionable age he wrote the stories of *The Lemon Table*, which concerns rage, old age, and death. At publication, Barnes, born in 1946, was still under 60.

When he was the other side of that milestone he published in 2008 the 'memoir', as the book jacket calls it, that serves as a non-fiction companion piece to *The Lemon Table*. A book about books, anecdotes, and thoughts about final things, as well as Barnes's own experiences of mortality, this meditation on the second death is pointedly entitled *Nothing to Be Frightened of*, echoing Arthur's first memory at the very start of *Arthur & George*, when he is shown his grandmother's corpse, perhaps 'to impress upon the child that death was nothing to be feared' (AG, p. 3).

That frightening 'Nothing', which Barnes says is the most exact, true, and meaningful word according to Renard (NF, p. 100 and p. 164), was first discussed as 'Big D' in *Metroland*. It is not so much the experience of dying that Christopher Lloyd fears in that novel, as what comes after: 'I wouldn't mind Dying at all, I thought, as long as I didn't end up Dead at the end of it' (M, p. 54). While in *Metroland* Christopher is for the most part privately tormented by any thought of eternal oblivion, at *The Lemon Table* death-talk is *de rigueur*. Taking his cue from the lemon's supposed representation of death in Chinese symbolism, Barnes's book is so called because he has demanded of himself that each story talks about the short-comings of old age in the expectation of an unhappy ending. We find in the final story, 'The silence', that the original Lemon Table was a convivial discussion group that Sibelius attended in a Helsinki restaurant in the 1920s, where it was 'obligatory – to talk about death' (LT, p. 206; NF, pp. 23–4).

Thus obliged to discuss death, Barnes's collection features several stories in which there are artists contemplating mortality, about which their art seems to provide little solace: ' "so much work, talent and courage, and then everything is over . . . To be misunderstood, and then to be forgotten, such is the artist's fate" ' (LT, p. 209), thinks Barnes's octogenarian Sibelius. The story ends with the composer calling for a lemon, having earlier declared that he wishes to have the slow movement of his Fourth Symphony played at his funeral and 'to be buried with a lemon clasped in the hand which wrote those notes' (LT, p. 211). 'The silence', evoking also Hamlet's dying words, has the last word on death in Barnes's second collection, charting connections between art and life, or silence and death, through music, just as 'Interference', about a fictionalised Delius trying to tune into BBC broadcasts of his compositions across *la manche*, stands as a suitably resonant opening to *Cross Channel*, providing an excellent metaphor for the place of (even English) art in French life and the miscommunications that pepper all Barnes's stories, whether on the subject of the Anglo-Saxons and the Gauls, men and women, or the old and the young.

Another of *The Lemon Table's* leitmotifs is sounded by the reference to Sibelius's Fourth Symphony. It seems the composition was referred to by one critic as a 'bark bread symphony', which alluded 'to the days when the poor used to adulterate flour with finely ground bark' (LT, p. 211). This is to say that for the critic Sibelius's music 'expressed a sullen and unpleasant view of life in general' (LT, p. 211). This resonates because 'Bark' is the title of one of the earlier stories in the collection: the narrative of a gourmand who gambles on outliving his peers, and subsequently finds sorrow and bitterness which result in a loss of appetite for life. Here again bark represents at best a resigned and at worst a sour negativity as a man for whom food has been a lifelong passion chooses and chews bark while others drink 'life-shortening concoctions' (LT, p. 129) that he thinks should mean they die before him. At the tale's conclusion, he finally gnaws miserably on a piece of bark while listening to his adult son's 'prattle' and 'idiocies' (LT, p. 136) and the man who has previously enjoyed reflecting 'contentedly on the folly of those around him' (LT, p. 123) dies with his linen nightcap in his hand, the equivalent of Sibelius's lemon.

Cross Channel has ten tales, each with a single-word title. *The Lemon Table* has only four one-word entitled stories among its eleven: 'Bark', plus 'Hygiene', 'Vigilance', and 'Appetite'. Intriguingly, 'Bark', itself referenced in 'The silence', mentions the title of each of the other three stories: 'the populace should be prompted to vigilance' (LT, p. 128); 'At the start it was simply a matter of hygiene' (LT, p. 132); 'He chewed on a sliver of tree bark, but without appetite' (LT, p. 136). These are thus cross-referencing stories that riff and play on some shared themes and phrases, but neither of Barnes's collections was conceived as an homogeneous whole like *A History of the World*.

'Bark' is set in nineteenth-century France and focuses on an elderly widower, Delacour, who falls for a young maid called Jeanne at the new bathhouse. He has employed Jeanne for sex, in which he has read it is healthy to indulge moderately. The bathhouse has been 'built as a matter of hygiene and general beneficence' by 40 subscribers, one of whom urges Delacour to 'renounce' his sexual arrangement; but Delacour is too much in love. 'Nothing in those experiences of my youth advised me of the possibility that carnal delight might lead to feelings of love. I imagined – no, I was sure – that it was always the other way round' (LT, p. 131). That Jeanne is the illegitimate daughter of the other subscriber who has urged his abstinence is also not something Delacour discovers until the man dies and Jeanne is pregnant. Delacour, who has spent his later life studying the law, concludes that the world is making 'less sense than it should' (LT, p. 135). Reason has not brought happiness: his gambling, which others thought a vice, 'seemed the application of a logical scrutiny to human behaviour', his gourmandism, which others saw as indulgence, 'seemed a rational approach to human pleasure' (LT, p. 136). Delacour has found that his rational approach to life is insufficient: 'we make such certainties as we can' (LT, p. 132) but nature and appetite make other choices. At the end of applying the rational exercise of free will to life, Delacour has no appetite left and he is discovered dead, having seemingly lost the will or the reason to live. Observing the inadequacy of his rationalism, he has concluded that, while he may have chosen how to approach his love of gambling, food and Jeanne, these were not desires that he chose to have. The corresponding section of *Nothing to Be Frightened of* conjectures that while 'we might think we are free in acting as we want, we cannot determine what it is that we want', and Barnes quotes Einstein's comment that 'a Being endowed with higher insight and more perfect intelligence . . . would smile about man's illusion that he was acting according to his own free will' (NF, p. 117).[3] Here as elsewhere the later memoir illuminates the earlier stories, not explaining them but revealing their concerns in fresh light.

Like 'Bark', 'The revival' is a story of renunciation and last love which also asks 'whether the heart drags in sex, or sex drags in the heart' (LT, p. 94). Barnes's protagonist is the writer Turgenev, whose viewpoint he has already noted in *Something to Declare* as 'after the age of forty, the basis of life is renunciation' (SD, p. 211; cf. NF, pp. 89–90). In 'The Revival', Turgenev is again 'a connoisseur of the if-only', and therefore a writer who favours the 'past-conditional' (LT, p. 95). Barnes here anatomises the fiction writer's preference for the conditional tense in opposition to the appetite of the twenty-first-century world for instant gratification and constant non-fictional actuality. In his story he also draws this contrast between the mystery and imaginings of 'love' and the numbers and consummation of 'sex'.

In *Nothing to Be Frightened of* Barnes reconsiders his own choice of the conditional in the light of his philosopher brother's suspicion and rejection of it. His brother sees the conditional as simply hypothetical, making the indulgence of it seem against reason. Barnes himself feels that the hypothetical – imagining what might or might have been the case – is a useful guide to action. Because indulging the conditional encourages us to act as we think others might want (instead of merely doing what we want), there is also an ethical dimension that impinges on the social contract's faith in reciprocity. So, when the undertaker asks Barnes if the religious symbols should be removed from the walls of the crematorium in which his mother lies, he answers that 'I thought that this is what she would have wanted' (NF, p. 5). His brother perceives this as a 'hypothetical want of the dead', doubly objectionable to the rationalist because it is both conjectural and passé: out of date because attributed to someone who no longer has preferences, let alone preferences upon which it might be possible to speculate. Barnes believes his brother thinks we can only do what we want and 'to indulge the maternal hypothetical was as irrational as if he were to pay attention to his own past desires' (NF, p. 6).

The indulgence of past and passed desires is one of the subjects of 'The revival' and part of the storywriter's stock-in-trade. Here, the past-conditional has a particular appeal of safety: 'The alluring hypothetical does not refer to the future' though Turgenev also 'had another tactic: that of hurrying into the future in order to confirm the impossibility of love in the present' (LT, p. 93). Avoiding reality, avoiding the present, is also what the novelist does, inasmuch as the hypothetical is stock-in-trade. But for Barnes this is the way in which the fiction writer approaches the truth, in imitation of the fabulist and the seeming safety of the merely conjectural: 'art, of course, is only a beginning, only a metaphor' (NF, p. 57). Barnes argues that the novel as a genre 'tells beautiful, shapely lies which enclose hard, exact truths' (NF, p. 78), suggesting that, through the suspension of disbelief, writer and reader are better able to explore aspects of life and death by avoiding a preoccupation with facts. Barnes's understanding of 'truth' is here not absolutist (cf. his discussion of religion: 'A beautiful, shapely story telling hard, exact lies' (NF, p. 78)) but relativist, perceiving art as telling 'more truth than anything else', and truth as something that 'can save us – up to a point – that's to say, enlighten us, move us, elevate us, even heal us' (NF, p. 75). Barnes also realizes that this is not a rationalist truth – it is an emotional one – which he explores through fiction. That he does this studiously and allusively has somewhat ironically led to the common view that he is a writer who inspires limited emotional engagement, tending to talk about love and art without eliciting the reader's affective investment in his often cerebral stories.[4]

Another facet to Barnes's interest in truth as opposed to fact is once more his take on memory. While his brother Jonathan, the philosopher, is portrayed as distrusting the 'essential truth' of memories *per se*, Barnes distrusts the ways in which we colour them (NF, p. 29).[5] Some of this dispute hinges on different interests in objective and subjective truth. For Barnes as a novelist he 'is less interested in the exact nature of truth, more in the nature of the believers, the manner in which they hold their beliefs, and the texture of the ground between the competing narratives' (NF, p. 240). Barnes gives examples from three generations of his family's disputes over memory and truth, forgetting neither the links between memory and identity (see NF, pp. 140–1) nor the ends towards which truth may be put: 'fiction . . . uses lies to tell the truth and truth to tell lies' (NF, p. 240). Barnes consequently revisits his understanding of what the novelist does and concludes that fictionalising involves recording and manipulating different versions of stories he *doesn't* remember, echoing the start of *England, England*, where Martha Cochrane replies 'I don't remember' to the question ' "What's your first memory?" ' (EE, p. 3)

In line with this view of art, on *The Lemon Table's* final page Sibelius avers in 'The silence' that 'one may express the truth in more than one way' (LT, p. 212), which is inevitably linked to different ways of imagining, and indeed of remembering: 'My brother distrusts most memories. I do not mistrust them, rather I trust them as workings of the imagination, as containing imaginative as opposed to naturalistic truth. Ford Madox Ford could be a mighty liar, and a mighty truth-teller, at the same time, and in the same sentence' (NF, pp. 244–5). The novelist tells non-remembered, unremembered or misremembered stories, which none the less express truths. As Barnes remarks of the elderly English protagonist of the final story in *Cross Channel*, who has written 'the stories you have just read': 'What was he, finally, but a gatherer and sifter of memories: his memories, history's memories? Also, a grafter of memories, passing them on to other people' (CC, p. 210).

Arguably, the novelist in Barnes's world seems to work like the twice-told legend of the gunshots that are 'extra' in 'The story of Mats Israelson', and which tourists pay for in order 'to awaken the echoes' in the passages of the Falun mines (LT, p. 31 and p. 47). Many characters in *The Lemon Table*, from Sibelius in his Silence and Turgenev in his Revival, try to reawaken the echoes, usually unsuccessfully, just as Barnes reawakens stories from other writers and artists in order to mine the truths hidden between different versions or pastiches of the past. Or, as Barnes quotes Stravinsky as saying: ' "I wonder if memory is true, and I know that it cannot be, but that one lives by memory nonetheless and not by truth" ' (NF, p. 228).

   'The story of Mats Israelson', set in late nineteenth-century Sweden, is indebted to a real-life incident that was also used by the German Romantic E. T. A. Hoffmann (1776–1822) in his tale 'The mines of Falun'. This is a gothic narrative of a young sailor lured to the mines and later to his death, on the morning of his wedding, by an apparition of an old man who died in the mines on St John's Day over a hundred years ago and 'always prophesied that some calamity would happen as soon as the miners' impulse to work ceased to be sincere love for the marvellous metals and ores'.[6] The sailor's bride returns annually to the mines on her catastrophic wedding day, which is also St John's Day, and fifty years after the cave-in that killed her betrothed sees his corpse brought to the surface, beautifully preserved. Hoffmann's story was inspired, though the name is not mentioned, by the legend of Mats Israelson, whose preserved body was discovered in the Falun mines and identified by his would-be bride of several decades earlier. Barnes uses the story as the centerpiece of his protagonist Anders's attempts to engage the interest of Barbro Lindwall, but Anders tells the story of Mats Israelson badly and she has 'little imagination', though she 'would like to visit Falun' (LT, pp. 31–2). When Barbro decides not to meet Anders on one occasion for the sake of their reputations, their unspoken love is left to languish for many years, not least because both are married to others, and Anders resolves that like Mats he will 'remain frozen, preserved, at this moment' (NF, p. 35). Many years later, dying of cancer, he calls Barbro to his death bed in Falun to see what remains of an idealized and unexplored love. However, as in the Hoffmann story where the petrified young man 'crumbles into dust' in the arms of his aged, dying bride, Anders and Barbro discover their love cannot bear exposure to the light of day. In the case of Anders and Barbro this is because their mutual attraction cannot overcome their inability to communicate: he cannot convey his love as he could not get across the story of Mats Israelson and Barbro leaves him thinking that he has summoned her to him for sex on the false pretext that he is dying.

Despite the collection's overall sardonic take on the book's working title, 'rage and age', several stories also embrace more sanguine
attitudes and assert equanimity if not defiance before the dying of
the light (NF, p. 181). 'Knowing French' is composed of a series of
letters written over three years to 'Barnes' by an octogenarian lady.
Geoffrey Braithwaite writes in *Flaubert's Parrot* about the reader–
writer relationship: 'You expect something from me too, don't you?
It's like that nowadays. People assume they own part of you, on no
matter how small an acquaintance; while if you are reckless enough
to write a book, this puts your bank account, your medical records,
and the state of your marriage irrevocably into the public domain'
(FP, p. 86). Flaubert disagreed, and so does Barnes but he has
imagined a 'correspondence' after this fashion in 'Knowing French'.
The story also responds to Virginia Woolf's essay 'On not knowing
French' from 1929. In the essay Woolf argues that to know French
one needs to be familiar not just with the language but with the idioms,
nuances, and living vitality of its cultural usage. Woolf admires the
writing of Conrad in English, as a second language speaker, but
observes that it is deeply idiosyncratic, whereas 'to know a language
one must have forgotten it'. It is not enough to parrot the words and
phrases.

Forgetting and misremembering are never far from the surface
of Barnes's stories and this is true also of 'Knowing French'. On
18 February 1986, Sylvia Winstanley, after the synchronicity of reading *Flaubert's Parrot* and then observing a caged grey parrot through
someone's window, writes to a *Dr* Barnes from her perch in Pilcher
House. On 4 March, in response to one of Barnes's missing letters,
like those of Juliet Herbert to Flaubert, Winstanley asks 'So why did
you say you were a doctor?', suggesting she has read *Flaubert's Parrot*
as the work of Barnes not Braithwaite. She is a methodical reader,
like Braithwaite, and has come to the 'B' section of her library after
reading through the 'A' section, and is seemingly confusing ontological
planes at the age of 'rising eighty-one' (LT, p. 139). Winstanley refers
to the coming together in her experience of the real and the written
about parrot as 'Coincidence? Of course' (LT, p. 140). She addresses
Barnes as the narrator of *Flaubert's Parrot* and gently admonishes
him for Braithwaite's disbelief in coincidence, which she argues is a
simple occasional veridical fact of life and that his objection can apply
only to the attribution of (divine or supernatural) intention to coincidence (FP, p. 66). Her parrot on a perch has prompted her to 'chase
the writer' (FP, p. 12), in her own way, and Winstanley in her old

folkery (a term also used by Oliver in *Talking It Over*, TO, p. 96) is
concerned like Braithwaite about how we seize time: 'A parrot's perch
catches the eye. We look for the parrot. Where is the parrot? We still
hear its voice; but all we can see is a bare wooden perch. The bird
has flown' (FP, p. 60). What remains is the memory and the question: is a memory something you have or something you've lost?[7]

In the interstices of Sylvia's letters we find responses to com-
munications from Barnes that echo his perspective in *Nothing to Be
Frightened of* or statements in his novels where the principal consolation for mortality is the oxymoronic weak promise of temporary
immortality offered by art. Sylvia observes Christopher Lloyd's comment from *Metroland* quoted above, 'You write that you are not
afraid of dying as long as you don't end up dead as a result' (LT,
p. 153), but adds that her own problems are manifold. Not only is she
surrounded by the dying and those who ask 'Am I dead yet?', but
she is also without anyone to join her at the proverbial Lemon Table,
because 'There's nobody here to talk to about death' (LT, p. 153).
Barnes therefore fits this bill but is also someone who, unlike her
fellow 'incarcerees' (LT, p. 141), is neither deaf nor mad.

In a book that is against serenity, a comparatively timorous counterpart to Sylvia and her courage while staring death in the face is the
protagonist at the centre of *The Lemon Table*'s first story (LT, p. 21).
'A short history of hairdressing' concerns an 'ageing geezer . . .
afraid of sex' whose name, like Jean Serjeant's son in *Staring at the
Sun*, is Gregory. The story follows him from youth to senior citizenship
through his experiences at the 'Barnet Shop' (LT, p. 18), chronicling
the changes in his hirsuteness, which ends with 'long mattressy'
eyebrows but 'thinning hair he'd soon have to comb more carefully'
(LT, p. 16, p. 21). The story also records changes in his life, which
amount to little that he considers important because he is simply
'one who stayed at home, went to work, and had his hair cut. His
life, he admitted, had been one long cowardly adventure' (LT, p. 20).
In the third part of his story, Gregory, with two grown-up children,
has been married longer than his hairdresser has been alive, though
the story intimates that Gregory has hardly lived at all. Now, his one
act of rebellion, or 'timid victory', is to decline after forty years the
rear view of his 'short back and sides', achieving at least a 'Revolt
against the tyranny of the bloody mirror' (LT, p. 22, p. 3).

Challenging the signs of ageing and the promise of death may
be small rebellions, but that visceral and primal revolt against the

conditions of the universe is the fundamental driving force of Barnes's second story collection, and also of his later memoir. Barnes records how his very being is repulsed by the inevitability of total, eternal annihilation: it is a certainty in which all wants will be merely the future wishes of the dead and sooner or later forgotten. *The Lemon Table* does not despair at this however, because observing the capacity to exercise intelligence and humour forces us to realise that the only way to live is as if we were not going to die while forcing ourselves to sit at the lemon table periodically to reflect on the necessity and indeed the advantages of mortality, like Sylvia Winstanley, who puts forward as good a case for death and dying as Barnes is able to muster anywhere in *Nothing to Be Frightened of*:

> Main reasons for dying: it's what others expect when you reach my age; impending decrepitude and senility; waste of money – using up inheritance – keeping together brain-dead incontinent bag of old bones; decreased interest in The News, famines, wars, etc.; fear of falling under total power of Sgt. Major; desire to Find Out about Afterwards (or not?). (LT, p. 151)

That 'Barnes' in his stories or memoir cannot elsewhere provide a superior answer is not a shortcoming, merely a necessity for a non-believer. This is chiefly because, as he notes, death happens to us for no other reason than because the universe happens to us. Sylvia Winstanley also adumbrates her main reasons for not dying, but can think of nothing more than rebelling against the expectations of some and avoiding distress to others. She concludes that, distressing though it may be for all involved, there are more reasons for dying than not, and so death ought to be nothing to be frightened of.

It remained for Barnes's 2005 novel *Arthur & George* to explore this point at length in fiction the year after *The Lemon Table* was published. This is a novel about differences between thinking, believing, and knowing: themes that equally apply to detection and discussion at *The Lemon Table*. Arthur begins the novel as a child outside a room wanting to go in where his deceased grandmother lies and 'to see' death. He becomes in later life a child who still wants to see the dead as he strives to prove his mother's existence beyond the grave using spiritualism. After his demise, the story ends with another 'innocent', George, also wanting 'to see' into death, peering not through a door ajar but through binoculars at a distant stage, beyond a drawn-aside curtain.

Notes

1 Uncollected short stories include 'A self-possessed woman' (1975), 'On the terrace' (1981), 'One of a kind' (1982), 'The writer who liked Hollywood' (1982), 'Hamlet in the Wild West' (1994), 'Trespass' (2003) 'Marriage lines' (2007), 'East wind' (2008), '60/40' (2008) and 'Sleeping with John Updike' (2010).

2 Barnes to Freiburg, 'Novels come out of life, not out of theories', p. 38.

3 This is reminiscent of the discussion above of *A History of the World*: 'we must believe in love, just as we must believe in free will and objective truth' (HW, p. 246).

4 For example, on the BBC Newsnight panel discussion of *The Lemon Table*, Adam Mars-Jones comments that 'the stylistic range is broader than the emotional range', while Bonnie Greer notes: 'Again, they are beautifully constructed, but the colour and the tempo: it's all the same', *Newsnight Review*, 12 March 2004, http://news.bbc.co.uk/1/hi/programmes/newsnight/review/3513468.stm, updated Monday 15 March 2004 (accessed 10 April 2008).

5 Barnes at university 'gave up languages for philosophy, found myself ill-equipped for it, and returned reluctantly to French' (SD, p. 11).

6 The story can be found, for example, at the Horror Masters website, www.horrormasters.com/Text/a0353.pdf (accessed 11 April 2008).

7 This is the closing question of the 1988 Woody Allen (dir.) film *Another Woman*.

10

Conviction and prejudice:
Arthur & George

When is a door not a door? When it's ajar.

Anon

Arthur & George is a book about unlikely pairings and questionable divisions. It is a fiction about truth and relativity, perception and rationality, fear and authority. Drawing on the real-life investigation by Arthur Conan Doyle of a miscarriage of justice, it explores the borderlines of nationality and ethnicity, evidence and imagination, doubt and faith, fact and fiction, endings and beginnings. Above all, it underlines the power of narrative to weave a plot from scraps of unsubstantiated information, in which the key factors are conviction (a title Barnes preferred) and prejudice. These pairings hint at Barnes's toying with duality, especially the co-presence of rational and faith-based explanations of events in the novel. It is very much a work of fiction though Barnes spent two years researching the story behind his plot, which draws on many sources, staying truer to the documented Conan Doyle record than the known story of George Edalji's life.

An in-depth study of the Edalji case was published by Gordon Weaver in the year after Barnes's novel, and a detailed discussion of the historical record and Barnes's (lack of) fidelity to the 'facts' has been published in the journal *International Commentary on Evidence*.[1] This article is an intertext one almost feels Barnes could have penned himself in jest given his perennial interest in exposing, in Dominic Head's words, 'the unreliability of the historical account'.[2] Whether factual mistakes matter in fictional works is something Barnes, or rather Braithwaite, discusses at some length in Chapter Six of *Flaubert's Parrot*.

Part of the intrigue of *Arthur & George* is directed at the play on distinctions between fact and fabulation, and Barnes seems deeply sceptical throughout his fiction of the notion of an accurate version of events. I would like none the less to précis the sequence of historical events Barnes was concerned with when shaping the plot of the novel. George Edalji was born in 1876, two years after his parents married, and eight years before the family moved to the rural mining district of Great Wyrley in south Staffordshire when George's father Shapurji was appointed to the vicarage. Insulting graffiti were written up on village walls within months of their arrival, and, during the worst years of 1892 to 1895, these were followed by notes thrown in at windows, fake orders, false advertisements, anonymous letters addressed to various people about the family or signed in the Edaljis' name, plus the sudden appearance at the vicarage of a stolen key from Walsall Grammar School (not George's school). This campaign against the Edaljis ceased at the end of 1895. However, in February 1903 a horse owned by Joseph Holmes in Wyrley was attacked in South Staffordshire. The brutal slashing left the animal bleeding to death in great pain. In the ensuing months several similar crimes were committed in the surrounding area, on cows, sheep, and horses. From the start of July, the police began to receive letters about the attacks, most signed with invented names but some supposedly signed by a schoolboy from Walsall Grammar, William Greatorex. At this time George was working in a Birmingham practice as a solicitor, having graduated from a predecessor of Birmingham University called Mason College. He had by this time won law society prizes as well as written his 1901 book *Railway Law for the 'Man in the Train'*. George was arrested one morning in August 1903 after a pony was discovered to have been ripped a few hours earlier, and then put on trial for the attack in October. The jury were persuaded by the circumstantial evidence of boot prints, handwriting similarities, and the letters' reference to a 'Wyrley *gang*' which meant that other crimes and letters during the trial did nothing to prove George's innocence. The previous history of the Edaljis' persecution was not mentioned in court and a petition to the Home Office with ten thousand signatures, including hundreds of lawyers, was ineffectual. Only the series of articles Conan Doyle published in the *Daily Telegraph*, which were also reported around the world and later produced as pamphlets, had impact. Doyle made play of the racial element and linked George's case to the persecution in France of Dreyfus (AG, pp. 173, 238, 302–3, and 332–3), a young Jewish soldier whose innocence was championed by Émile Zola in his famous 1898 tract *J'Accuse*.[3]

The Home Secretary appointed a committee to review the case, and it found George Edalji not guilty of the crimes for which he had been convicted. However, the Committee did insist that George had written the letters, with the result that he was granted a pardon but offered no compensation, for the reason that he was considered to have invited his troubles. While the Law Society readmitted George to the roll of solicitors and the *Daily Telegraph* raised a subscription for him, Doyle had to embark upon a second bout of article writing and campaigning to clear George of writing the letters. On 27 January 1907, Arthur wrote to his mother that the real offenders were 'three youths (one already dead), brothers by the name of Sharp'.[4] Doyle, now the recipient of threatening letters, then drew up his private report for the Home Office, entitled 'The case against Royden Sharp for the committing of the outrages upon cattle from February to August 1903, for which George Edalji was condemned to seven years penal servitude at Stafford Assizes November 1903'. The response was that there was no *prima facie* case for the Sharps to meet. Doyle never named Royden Sharp publicly, while the Chief Constable of Staffordshire, Captain Anson, wrote publicly in Sharp's defence. George moved to London and practised law there until his death in 1953.

Around this story of one legal case, Barnes weaves two narratives: a story of George Edalji and another of Arthur Conan Doyle. The interaction between the two men is negligible in terms of the development of a relationship but their stories are woven together in ways that compare and contrast their lives as well as treating the real-life connection between them.

Arthur & George is framed as a book of endings and beginnings with a deep scepticism towards both, preferring the image of the door ajar to the certainty of the door closed or open. The novel's four parts advertise this arrangement in their titles and Barnes often enters into repeated discussion of the difficulties of starting points and conclusions. For example, a question is set in part two of the book: 'How can you make sense of the beginning if you don't know what the ending is?' (AG, p. 193). Arthur poses this query in terms of the possibility of an afterlife but it is made clear in the novel that this is his habitual way of working. An answer is given to his enquiry much later by Captain Anson, the police Chief Constable, in Part Three of the novel: 'Because, Doyle, you cannot understand the ending until you know the beginning' (AG, p. 274). Anson refers to an interview Doyle gave in the *Strand* some years ago, saying: ' "You described how, when you wrote your tales, that it was always the conclusion which first preoccupied you." Conan Doyle replies: "Beginning with an ending. You cannot know which path to travel unless you first know the destination" ' (AG, p. 267). The interview referred to is 'A Day with Dr Conan Doyle' from *The Strand Magazine: An Illustrated Monthly* in August 1892.[5] The interviewer Harry How writes: 'Dr Doyle invariably conceives the end of his story first, and writes up to it. He gets the climax, and his art lies in the ingenious way in which he conceals it from his readers.'[6] There is a suggestion here that Conan Doyle therefore sees life also this way and the attraction of spiritualism is that it will give him an ending beyond death. It also however reflects on the nature of evidence and court proceedings, where truth is subservient to that which the jury can be persuaded to believe: the vital ingredient in securing a conviction is conviction.

Barnes's novel begins with a young Arthur Conan Doyle *wanting to see* the corpse of his dead grandmother, which becomes his first memory. The novel ends with George Edalji, assisted by binoculars, trying to see the shade of the recently deceased Arthur in a vacant chair at the Royal Albert Hall after a spiritualist has declared his presence on stage: 'the one specific empty chair with its cardboard placard, the space where Sir Arthur has, just possibly, been' (AG, p. 357).

To a degree, Barnes is playing with the approach that Conan Doyle used both for his fiction and for his detective work. 'As he set to work, Arthur felt back on familiar ground. It was like starting a book: you had the story but not all of it, most of the characters but not all of them some but not all of the causal links. You had your beginning, and you had your ending' (AG, p. 237). Arthur then proceeds to write a fifteen-thousand-word report which begins like a novel: 'The first sight which I ever had of Mr. George Edalji was enough in itself both to convince me of the extreme improbability of his being guilty . . .' (AG, p. 256). When he meets Captain Anson, his report is first deemed not an 'analysis', Arthur's word, but a 'story', and when the term 'analysis' is allowed Anson qualifies it by describing the report as 'amateur speculations' (AG, p. 266).[7] The same accusation might be levelled at Conan Doyle's belief in spiritualism, but that is an ending that can be understood only by knowing the start of his story.

The title of the first part of *Arthur & George* is thus 'Beginnings' and in this comparatively short forty-page backstory Barnes establishes the major concerns and themes of the book: romance fiction, births, marriages, and deaths, the emergence of Sherlock Holmes, adventure, detection, class, race, and a host of others. It also contains clues for the legal case at the heart of the story, including in passing, 250 pages before his real name appears, the supposed villain of the narrative: Royden Sharp (ward of Mr Greatorex and son of his tenant farmer) mentioned by his forensically resonant nickname 'Speck' (AG, p. 41, pp. 285–97). Sharp is cited as the perpetrator of a crime on the railway – smashing a window – of which others are accused, presaging George's interest in railway law ('George finds himself increasingly preoccupied by the civil connection between passengers and the railway company', AG, p. 51), which develops a few pages later at the beginning of the second part.

Here, the first hoax letters denouncing George as part of a gang claim to be sent by a Walsall Grammar schoolboy called Greatorex, whom George has in fact encountered on his train rides to work (AG, pp. 74, 80, 89, 101). And, as noted above, it is with regard to trains that violence of the kind later inflicted on horses and cattle is first contemplated: 'George feels quietly enraged when anyone seeks to harm the railway. There are youths – men, perhaps – who take knives and razors to the leather window straps' (AG, p. 50). This thought, which spurs George's interest in railway law, provides a bridge between Speck's vandalism and the later horse mutilations which Inspector Campbell thinks are done not with a knife but with a razor (AG, p. 77).

To underline the possible links – whether telepathic, coincidental, or premeditated – the first mention of 'Speck' and the railway-carriage window incident in the narrative, which happened shortly before the initial threatening letters arrived, is followed by a statement that goes to the heart of Barnes's narrative concerns in *Arthur & George*: 'Perhaps there was some connection. Perhaps not' (AG, p. 41). As I mentioned above, Sharp is not identified as the perpetrator of the crimes for another 250 pages, at which point Arthur notes: 'It's not meant to happen like this, . . . I should know. I've written it enough times. It's not meant to happen by following simple steps. It's meant to seem utterly insoluble right up until the end. And then you unravel the knot with one glorious piece of deduction, something entirely logical yet quite astounding' (AG, p. 293). On the next page, Arthur is described as feeling as he does when he nears the end of writing a book. As for George, the fact that Conan Doyle is writing about him, and in the newspapers, makes him feel 'like several over-lapping people at the same time: a victim seeking redress; a solicitor facing the highest tribunal in the country; and a character in a novel' (AG, p. 297). When the Home Office report is produced, Arthur indeed describes it as a 'novella' (AG, p. 308). Meanwhile, George had wanted to make his reputation as a lawyer but has become famous as a miscarriage of justice.

The sections of 'Beginnings' take the focalised approach of James Joyce's *A Portrait of the Artist as a Young Man*, using a third-person narrator who mostly employs the language and vocabulary of the character at that age: 'He is not sure he likes coal. It is smelly and dusty and noisy when poked, and you are told to keep away from its flames' (AG, p. 7). Generally the narrator adopts a flat, descriptive tone, but later in the novel there are some signs of a narrative personality that bears Barnes's characteristically ironic tone, as when the common misunderstanding of George's Parsee father's origins infiltrates an otherwise simple statement: 'The prisoner's father, the Hindoo Vicar of Great Wyrley, also gave evidence' (AG, p. 115).[8]

The first part of the book is presented in short sections alternately describing the early years of the two main characters, who are in complete ignorance of each other. Barnes uses Arthur's first remembered moment of entering a room to see his grandmother's corpse as a way into imagining the seeds of Conan Doyle's interest in spiritualism and his desire to see whether there is any continuation after death. This interest grows throughout the book though Conan Doyle cannot speak about it to his beloved mother ('he can never allude to his deepening interest in spiritualism, or spiritism as he prefers it', AG, p. 191) or to the woman he comes to love, Jean Leckie, who is suspicious and somewhat frightened of 'anything touching the psychic world' (AG, p. 191).[9]

Placed in a third position that differs from Arthur's and Jean's, George is in large part resistant to spiritism because he 'lacks imagination' (AG, p. 4).[10] Indeed George has been led by his parents to associate 'too much imagination' with fibs, tall stories, and at worst lies. At the Vicarage where they live, the truth is always expected yet the book goes on to illustrate how the 'eyes of faith' (AG, p. 355) are linked to imagination. Brought up on the truth of the Word, George has little capacity for imagination and cannot see how to believe in the spiritualism experiment; Arthur by contrast has an excess of imagination and cannot distinguish truth from wish-fulfilment. Arthur as a boy knows the Bible is 'the truth' but his imagination prefers the romance stories his mother tells him in the kitchen, and which are connected to the extra commandments she teaches him on top of the Mosaic ten: ' "Fearless to the strong; humble to the weak", was one, and "Chivalry towards women, of high and low degree" ' (AG, p. 5). Arthur is enthralled by his mother, but his father is dismissed as a 'gentle failure' of a man, a sentimental drunk: 'what he liked to paint

best, and was most remembered for painting, was fairies' (AG, p. 8).[11]
George's parents provide a far more ordinary family setting unequi-
vocally rooted in Christian principles: 'There is Mother, who is constantly present in his life, teaching him his letters, kissing him
goodnight; and Father, who is often absent because he is visiting the
old and the sick, or writing his sermons, or preaching them' (AG,
p. 6). Arthur travels a great deal and leads an expansive life; George
knows only the Vicarage and is bemused by the most ordinary things
in the world outside, from cows to schoolboys.

Barnes thus contrasts the two boys' experiences of growing up, in
terms of family, school, religion, attitudes, and aptitudes. Differences
and similarities are additionally drawn between them in direct ways
– such as their chosen professions of doctor and lawyer – but there
are also roundabout comparisons: Arthur believes the heart of
Englishness lies in the romance of the fourteenth century but for
the Edaljis it is the Church of England that provides the lifeblood of
England's Empire; George has a habit of referring to those whose
behaviour he doesn't understand as 'loonies' and Arthur's father is
transferred to a lunatic asylum while George is encouraged to plead
insanity by the police – 'You want me to say I am loony' (AG, p. 107);[12]
George is delighted when 'given the opportunity to play the detective'
(AG, p. 22), while Arthur later invents a world-famous one; Arthur
determines to become an ophthalmologist, whereas George is so short-
sighted he cannot see the school blackboard and in his humiliation
soils himself repeatedly. While Arthur has a 'way of popularity' (AG,
p. 11) in his story-telling and develops a confident sense of himself
through challenges and adversity (as with his first experience of rank
injustice when Edinburgh University withdraws his bursary following a bureaucratic error, AG, p. 21), George is portrayed early on as
a victim of serial persecutions: at school, at the hands of a maid;
through the malicious hoaxes that plague his family; and most
alarmingly by the police. Arthur, for whom there is a 'mystery of the
victim' (AG, p. 236), is thus presented as George's potential saviour
long before they meet: 'chivalry was the prerogative of the powerful
. . . honour was a living thing for which you should be prepared
to die' (AG, p. 23). Arthur's posthumous 'appearance' at his own
memorial service near the end of the book sees him greeted like a
redeemer and underscores this thematic strand. 'Saviour' is the
word George ascribes to him (AG, p. 354), which the reader understands from these beginnings in terms of Arthur's romantic chivalry

and his desire to save not only himself but the whole world through discovering true spiritism.

The first part's charting of disparate beginnings self-consciously ends when the initial set of hoaxes ceases. Partly for this reason, the second part is entitled 'Beginning with an Ending', but the phrase itself does not appear in the narrative until two hundred pages later when Arthur makes the pronouncement that knowing the destination is the key to knowing which 'path to travel' (AG, p. 267). This is in the conversation Arthur has with Anson, mentioned above. Anson here argues that this is also the way Conan Doyle has approached the Edalji case, basing all his investigation on his conviction that the endpoint to be arrived at is George's innocence, of which Arthur became convinced as soon as he set eyes on him, thus beginning with an ending once more. His instinct has guided him, rather than logic. It would be easy also to extrapolate from this a critique of the Holmes stories, where Conan Doyle's detective is repeatedly proved right even though his deductive logic is highly speculative.

The second part's first sentence also introduces a story-telling conceit as the narrator makes an assertion and then corrects it, seemingly emphasising how the most authoritative account can be misremembered. The amendment is to a factual statement about how long Sharpuji Edalji has been in his parish ('the twentieth – no, the twenty-first – Christmas celebrated at the vicarage': AG, p. 49), and the correction is thus perhaps Shapurji's, but may be the narrator's. The hint of narratorial unreliability here arguably highlights that all the story is focalised though character witnesses, or at least that it is being presented after the manner of a testimony. The effect is heightened by the importance given, for example, to keys: a key from Walsall School is left outside the vicarage and George finds it (AG, pp. 30–1); George has a railway carriage key as a paperweight in his office, which Inspector Campbell jokes is a pistol (AG, p. 99); George sleeps in the same room as his father, who locks the bedroom each night but also leaves the key in the door (AG, p. 104).

'Beginning with an Ending' moves forward several years after the hoaxes to the time of the animal assaults for which George becomes the main police suspect from August to October 1903 (AG, p. 226). This part also introduces variants on the strictly alternating 'Arthur' and 'George' sections from Part One, including some sections entitled 'Campbell' after the Inspector who investigates the animal mutilations. Though such sections sometimes include the thoughts of others, the first of them that is not actually focused on Arthur or George is the short interjection that describes one of the horse mutilations. It is headed 'George and Arthur' as though suggesting that, because the assailant is not to be named, the section can be identified as the initiation of the 'case' that brings Edalji and Conan Doyle together. It also marks the phase of the novel that is concerned with the police investigation into the crimes, and Conan Doyle does not figure again for nearly a hundred pages.

When Arthur does reappear, his parallel situation to George's trial case is his undeclared relationship with Jean while his wife Touie, an 'invalid' with consumption, is still alive. Though he hates lies, Arthur comes to terms with his double life, which he feels remains respectable but which his family find 'compromising' in a way that parallels how George has been discredited: 'There is always the tattle of maids and servants. People write anonymous letters. Journalists drop hints in newspapers' (AG, p. 177). Arthur feels as though he is in the Zugzwang chess position: 'the player is unable to move any piece in any direction to any square without making his imperiled state worse' (AG, p. 197). Jean for her part realises after ten years that she does not wish to play a secondary role in Arthur's life for ever: 'She has been Arthur's waiting girl since March the fifteenth 1897; in a few months it will be the tenth anniversary of their meeting' (AG, p. 222). A parallel is also drawn unwittingly by Anson when he says to Arthur about George: 'When would he ever achieve any kind of sexual fulfilment? In my view, a continuous period of sexual frustration, year after year after year, can start to turn a man's mind, Doyle. He can end up worshipping strange gods, and performing strange rites' (AG, p. 279). This refers to the fact that George has always shared a locked bedroom at night with his father, but for Arthur it reminds him of his own sexless years of marriage to Touie and his turn to spiritualism.

This turn is also precipitated by the extra commandments Arthur has learned from his mother. It is his 'Mama' who persuades him to accept a knighthood when he thinks such honours are fit for 'a provincial city mayor'. Arthur previously resisted the award, even though his childhood dreams were of knights of chivalry, because he thinks his heroes Rhodes, Chamberlain, and Kipling would not accept such a bauble (AG, p. 185). There would thus appear to be in his mind a division between the medieval knights to whose stature he aspires, and others' modern pretensions to be called 'Sir': hence

Jean has inscribed on his gravestone 'BLADE STRAIGHT, STEEL TRUE. A sportsman and a chivalrous knight to the end' (AG, p. 326). Similarly, Arthur feels that *The White Company* and *Sir Nigel* are his 'best writings' (AG, p. 326), even though they are treated by reviewers eager for the modern detective work of Holmes as adventure-tales appropriate for boys. For Arthur, his historical novels depict a way of life driven by noble principles. As noted by one of Conan Doyle's biographers, in *Sir Nigel* (1905) the chivalric hero is instructed on 'the emptiness of sordid life, the beauty of heroic death, the high sacred-ness of love and the bondage of honour', intimating the code that Barnes's Conan Doyle seeks to live by and the romantic ideals that underpin his perspective on life, love, and the significance of mort-ality when, as quoted above, 'honour was a living thing for which you should be prepared to die' (AG, p. 23).[13]

When receiving his knighthood at the Palace from the new king, Arthur's interest in spiritualism is spurred by meeting Sir Oliver Lodge, a professor who has retired as president of the Physical Society now to become president of the Psychical Society: 'the two new Edwardian knights talk about telepathy, telekinesis and the reliabil-ity of mediums' (AG, p. 186). Arthur avers soon after that: 'The whole point of psychical research . . . is to eliminate and expose fraud and deceit' (AG, p. 194). It is another instance of detective work and sci-entific deduction based on a conviction derived from feeling rather than evidence: 'We need only prove it once and it is proved for every-body and for all time' (AG, p. 195).

Perhaps the most idiosyncratic aspect to the novel becomes appar-ent in the second part. Barnes's use of tenses insinuates the focal points of interest at any point, which is not concerned only with causality but with the relationship between the past, present and the future. Throughout the first part of the novel Arthur's story is told in the past tense while sections concerning George, who is sixteen years younger, are all in the present. This continues into the second part, with other sections (e.g. Campbell's and the 'George & Arthur' section) taking the past tense. Only after the story of George's court ordeal (consecutive sections starting with the same heading, 'George', on George's trial and imprisonment that last over sixty pages), does a section concerning Arthur adopt the present tense for the first time.

This section concludes the second part of the book and fills in the story of Arthur's life while George is imprisoned, charting the nine years from his first meeting with Jean, through Touie's death from tuberculosis in July 1906, to his first encounter with the name George Edalji. It is Arthur's story that now seems to take the dominant currency of the present tense as the two stories coincide in time, with the centre of gravity also shifting to the consequences of his decision to take on George's case after receiving a package containing cuttings from *The Umpire*, a Birmingham newspaper of which Arthur has not heard, but which successfully plugs into his sense of fair play, epitomised by his love of cricket.

The sections of the third part use both past and present as the narrative is taken from telling to showing: from elucidation and description though to the protagonists' first meeting and subsequent conversations. When the story moves to a section headed 'Anson' (AG, p. 261) the tense changes again to the past and 'Arthur' is more often referred to as 'Doyle.' The theme of belief and conviction in relation to truth is intensified in this section:

> How easily everyone understood what was real and what was not. The world in which a benighted young solicitor was sentenced to penal servitude in Portland . . . the world in which Holmes unravelled another mystery beyond the powers of Lestrade and his colleagues . . . or the world beyond, the world behind the closed door, through which Touie had effortlessly slipped. Some people believed in only one of these worlds, some in two, a few in all three. Why did people imagine that progress consisted in believing in less, rather than believing in more, in opening yourself to more of the universe? (AG, p. 265)

When the section titles become 'George and Arthur' (AG, p. 297) 'Arthur and George' (AG, p. 305) and 'George and Arthur' again (AG, p. 315), it is the perspective of the first named in each section that takes the present tense, while the second named takes the past. This technique is partly justified by the fact that, up to Arthur's wedding to Jean, he and George have met only twice (AG, p. 319). Most intriguingly the novel ends with a chapter whose first half is in the past tense and whose second half is in the present; it concludes, as does the novel, with three questions, all in different tenses: 'What does he see? What did he see? What will he see?' (AG, p. 357). As Barnes has said in interview: 'My books are about posing the questions in the right way and not giving answers.'[14] But this toying with tenses illustrates the book's interest in the interaction between past, future, and present, intertwining beginnings and endings.

These are also questions that might be applied to the novel's beginning when the questions concern young Arthur and his first

memory: a primal moment of curiosity-driven detection, 'the instinc-
tive tourism of infancy' when he strives to see the corpse of his elderly
relative. Doyle's Cartesian dualism is expressed in this inaugural scene
of separation when 'Grandmother's soul had clearly flown up to heaven,
leaving behind only the sloughed husk of her body' (AG, p. 3); an
incident that encapsulates the twin foci of Doyle's autobiography
Memories and Adventures. When rereading this volume, prompted by
Arthur's death, George is dismayed again by the *beginning* of Doyle's
story about his 'case' which implies he believes his interest in George
to have been prompted by the death of Touie, which cast Arthur into
despondency:

> 'In 1906,' he read yet again, 'my wife passed away after a long illness
> . . . For some time after these days of darkness I was unable to settle
> to work until the Edalji case came suddenly to turn my energies into
> an entirely unexpected channel.' George always felt a little uneasy at
> this beginning. It seemed to imply that his case had come along at a
> convenient moment, its peculiar nature being just what was required
> to drag Sir Arthur from a slough of despond; as if he might have reacted
> differently – indeed, not at all – had the first Lady Conan Doyle not
> recently died. Was this being unfair? (AG, p. 335)[15]

In contrast to the growing inclination towards a rationalised spiritism
in Doyle's life-story, Barnes's logical scepticism is often given free
rein. This is the side that leans towards syllogistic rationality as well
as philosophical reflection. In many places it is revealed through
catechistic inquiries, in and out of court, as for example in Arthur's
cross-examination of Dr Butter, the police surgeon who gave evidence
in court (AG, pp. 250–5). Butter's professional scientific opinion is
forcefully underlined by his reliance on neither inclination nor belief
but a verifiable evidence base:

> 'I have worked with the Staffordshire Constabulary for twenty years
> and more . . . twenty years of presenting evidence which is as clear and
> unambiguous as I can make it, which is based on rigorous scientific
> analysis, and then being treated, if not as a fraud, then as someone who
> is merely giving an opinion, that opinion being no more valuable than
> the next man's except that the next man does not have a microscope
> and if he did would not be competent to focus it. I state what I have
> observed – what I know – and find myself being told disdainfully that
> this is merely what I happen to think.' (AG, p. 255)

One of the significances of this is to point up the involvement of
prejudice in the Edalji case, which parallels the Dreyfus scandal

championed by Zola in France. To an extent, Barnes's initial interest
in the Edalji investigation and trial derives from the comparison, allowing him to develop questions of national and ethnic belonging that
were largely obscured by the focus of *England, England* on heritage
culture.

After his investigation, Arthur publishes his 'Statement of the
Case against Royden Sharp'. To George, 'the case against' is weak
because he does not know Sharp, though he thinks he must have
been at school with Sharp's brother. In fact, when the letters recom-
mence at the time of the mutilations, a phrase used by one letter writer,
and queried by the police, is that people think George is not 'a right
sort' (AG, pp. 83, 85). George only takes this to be a reference to his
father's Parsee family background, apparently not remembering that
this is a phrase that was used against him at school by a boy called
Wallie Sharp (AG, p. 9), brother of Royden 'Speck' Sharp.

To Arthur there is a fundamental prejudicial motivation behind
the persecution of George that has started with Sharp and continued
throughout the subsequent proceedings. However, George demurs
from this point of view:

> 'I am aware that you consider race prejudice to be a factor in the case,
> Sir Arthur. But as I have already said, I cannot agree. Sharp and I do
> not know one another. To dislike someone you have to know them.
> And then you find the reason for disliking them. And then, perhaps,
> if you cannot find a satisfactory reason, you blame your dislike on some
> oddity of theirs, such as the colour of their skin.' (AG, p. 301)

Here, the two protagonists' inclinations towards imagination and a
metaphorical myopia are foregrounded. Arthur 'thinks that you can
only point to the obvious so many times' (AG, p. 301) while George,
deriving his opinion from direct experience, thinks simply that for
circumstantial reasons the 'police were prejudiced against him from
the start' (AG, p. 307). He also concludes that by stealing the horse
lancet and having no solid evidence against Royden Sharp, Arthur
has 'destroyed the legal case against Sharp even as he was trying to
make it'. In effect, he is inclined to blame Doyle's fantasy world of
Holmes for undermining the evidence base that might have exoner-
ated him (AG, pp. 304–5).

Arthur's written case for George's exoneration is lodged with the
Home Office, who produce their report on the Friday before Whitsun
in 1907. George is found innocent of the attacks but guilty of 'impish

mischief' in supposedly writing the letters. Consequently, a pardon
is granted but no compensation offered. Arthur is aghast:

> 'this England of ours has discovered a new legal concept. In the old
> days, you were either innocent or guilty. If you were not innocent, you
> were guilty, and if you were not guilty, you were innocent. A simple
> enough system, tried and tested down many centuries, grasped by judges,
> juries and the populace at large. As from today, we have a new concept
> in English law – guilty *and* innocent.' (AG, p. 310)

Questions are asked in Parliament, finishing with a speculation that
underlines Barnes's interest in the parallel case of the Alsace-born
Dreyfus, persecuted because he was seen as Jewish but not French:
'Is Edalji being thus treated because he is not an Englishman?' (AG,
p. 314). The case then fails to generate further publicity and it is only
left for Jean to suggest that Arthur invites George to their wedding
reception, where 'The unofficial Englishman looks at his unofficial
fiancé' (AG, p. 315). George also concludes he has been found innocent yet guilty:

> so said the Gladstone Committee, and so said the British Government
> through its Home Secretary. Innocent yet guilty. Innocent yet wrong-
> headed and malicious. Innocent yet indulging in impish mischief.
> Innocent yet deliberately seeking to interfere with the proper investi-
> gations of the police. Innocent yet bringing his troubles upon himself.
> Innocent yet undeserving of compensation. Innocent yet undeserv-
> ing of an apology. Innocent yet fully deserving of three years' penal
> servitude. (AG, p. 316)

Though he does not actually conceive of the writing of Barnes's novel,
George allows his mind to stretch towards postulating vindication in
posterity and 'to imagine a legal textbook written a hundred years hence'
(AG, p. 317). The Criminal Court of Appeal is at least established by
the case, and that is something George can take a small comfort in
as a solicitor.

That a greater commotion has not been made, as happened in France
over the Dreyfus case, is something that George ascribes to the
national character: 'This was England, and George could understand
England's point of view, because George was English himself' (AG,
p. 333). Yet, George has also declined to see the racial element in his
case that Arthur sees, and he remains convinced that this is not something to which Conan Doyle should draw attention, though Arthur
even makes a point of it in his autobiography: '"the appearance of a

coloured clergyman with a half-caste son in a rude, unrefined parish was bound to cause some regrettable situation"' (AG, p. 335).

This statement from *Memories and Adventures* points up once more the differences between Arthur, an insider who sees himself as an outsider in England, and George, an outsider who sees himself as an insider. On the one hand there is George's religious upbringing. On the other, Arthur sees the Church of England as a factor in the worst aspects of the case and an enemy of the truth of spiritism. Thus, the fact that the individual who writes the letters that Arthur calls 'noxious effusions' signs them as 'Satan' leads Arthur to conclude: 'God Satan: how peculiarly repellent were the perversions of an institutional religion once it began its irreversible decline. The sooner the whole edifice was swept away the better' (AG, p. 228). Again, while Arthur is influenced by his father, but also ashamed of him as the family disgrace, George is positioned in religious terms by his father, who grew up in India, converted to Christianity as a youth, and came to occupy a quintessential English position of vicar in a country village: 'My father, you must understand, believes that this new century will bring in a more harmonious commingling of the races than in the past – that this is God's purpose, and I am intended to serve as some kind of messenger. Or victim. Or both' (AG, p. 214). For Arthur, even 'Jesus was a highly trained mystic' (AG, p. 194), and his imagination is fired by a less orthodox belief, inspired by his mother's childhood stories:

> 'I agree with your father that this new century is likely to bring extraor-
> dinary developments in man's spiritual nature . . . Man is on the verge
> of elaborating the truths of psychical law as he has for centuries been
> elaborating the truth of physical law. When these truths come to be
> accepted, our whole way of living – and dying – will have to be
> rethought from first principles.' (AG, p. 214)

And while George does not believe racial prejudice lies behind his ordeal (AG, p. 216),[16] Arthur coins a new expression to unite their causes: 'You and I, George, you and I, we are . . . unofficial Englishmen' (AG, p. 217).[17] This is a comment George finds ambiguous and somewhat perplexing for many reasons, not least because 'My father brought me up an Englishman' (AG, p. 218).[18]

'Ending with a Beginning' concludes with George's attendance at Arthur and Jean's wedding reception at the Hotel Metropole on 18 September 1907. The fourth and final, short part is 'Endings', and it begins twenty-three years later with news of Arthur's death at the age of seventy-one. This part has only one section, entitled 'George', and focuses on a public farewell to Sir Arthur at the Albert Hall, to be organised by the secretary of the Marylebone Spiritualist Association and to include 'a demonstration of clairvoyance' (AG, p. 327).

Before entering the hall, George visits the Albert Memorial, which evokes thoughts of final things, standing for him as an emblem of passings: of the Victorian era, of Prince Albert and of Arthur Conan Doyle. '[N]earing the limit of his imagination', George considers how,

> If you knew someone who had died, then you could think about them in one of two ways: as being dead, extinguished utterly, with the death of the body the test and proof that their self, their essence, their individuality, no longer existed; or you could believe that somewhere, somehow, according to whatever religion you held, and how fervently or tepidly you held it, they were still alive, either in a way predicted by sacred texts, or in some way we had yet to comprehend. It was one or the other; there was no position of compromise. (AG, p. 340)

Speaking to the theme of duality in the novel, mentioned at the start of this chapter, the passage points up how human affairs admit of positions of compromise, and this appears to highlight Doyle's accusation of British justice when a logical contradiction, or seeming paradox, is also the official decision on George's case. To be both innocent and guilty appears to be the final verdict in a story of ambiguities, equivocations, irresolutions, and questions without clear answers. Another example is the matter of Arthur's relationship with Jean over the many years he was married to Touie, which may or may not have been adulterous but was in many respects simultaneously known and unacknowledged both privately and publicly. A further instance of national compromise is illustrated when we learn that George himself inclines towards 'extinction' as the more probable answer to his question of what happens after death, but he will 'doubtless' carry on 'observing like the rest of the country . . . the general rituals of the Church of England' (AG, p. 340). To an extent, beside the values of honour and truth that the protagonists believe in, compromise, prejudice, and indeed hypocrisy appear to be quintessences of Englishness in the novel.

When he tries to get a better view of the Albert Hall stage and Arthur's empty chair, George is told that his binoculars will not help him: 'You will only see him with the eyes of faith' (AG, p. 355). As

he looks for signs of Arthur's presence, George himself is unable to
decide what he is seeing, and 'does not know whether he has seen
truth or lies, or a mixture of both. He does not know if the clear,
surprising, unEnglish fervour of those around him this evening is
proof of charlatanry or belief. And if belief, whether true or false' (AG,
p. 356). This echoes George's inability to see the board as a schoolboy
as he peers from the back of the class, and seems to conclude a theme
in the book of George's inability or unwillingness to 'see' things, which
would include the element of racial prejudice in his persecution,
whereas Arthur sees too much. It also takes the novel back to the
opening scene of Arthur wanting to 'see' his grandmother when there
is only a corpse to be found. His grandmother had become a 'white,
waxen thing' at the moment that Arthur himself came to forge a first
memory and become a conscious individual with memories, ceasing
to be akin to a 'thing'.

The book concludes with an Author's Note, which observes that
four years after Arthur's death a labourer called Enoch Knowles
pleaded guilty to writing 'menacing letters over a thirty-year period'
(AG, p. 359). The note quotes from an article George wrote for the
Daily Express in the same year, 1934; however, his conclusion is no
conclusion at all: 'The great mystery, however, remained unsolved.
All kinds of theories were advanced' (AG, p. 360).[19]

As also intimated by the duality of the title, this is an anti-Holmes
novel that stresses different viewpoints but also undecidability, irre-
solution, and loose ends – like the unsolved murder of Sophie
Hickman or the murders of Jack the Ripper, as well as the animal
mutilations for which no one was found responsible. It arguably therefore positions itself as a novel of Edwardian shifts from Victorian
certainties prior to general understanding of the theories of relativity that were to pervade science and culture after the Great War.

As I mentioned at the start of this chapter, *Arthur and George*
is also a meditation on the relationship between fact and fiction.
Published a few years before Barnes's novel, Daniel Stashower's
biography of Doyle notes that,

> As more than one newspaper commented, it seemed as if Sherlock
> Holmes himself has rallied to Edalji's defence. Conan Doyle brushed
> aside the suggestion: 'There is a good deal of difference between fact
> and fiction,' he told the *Daily Telegraph*, 'but I have endeavoured to get
> at facts first before coming to any conclusion.' Indeed, Conan Doyle's
> efforts more closely resembled those of Mycroft Holmes, the detective's

older, less ambulatory brother. Most of the facts had been assembled
by others, but Conan Doyle used his narrative gifts to cast the evidence
into a compelling and seemingly unanswerable argument. He began
with a letter-writing campaign in the newspapers and then, in late January
1907, published an eighteen-thousand-word pamphlet called 'The Story
of Mr. George Edalji' . . . Recent investigations suggest that the final
chapter of the Edalji case has yet to be written. 'He was of irreproach-
able character,' Conan Doyle insisted. 'Nothing in his life had ever been
urged against him.' Subsequent research indicates that Edalji may not
have been entirely pure of heart. Rumours of gambling debts and mis-
appropriation of client funds have surfaced, indicating that the story may
have a final twist. As a 1907 editorial in the *New York Times* noted, '[Conan
Doyle] may have been misled by the literary artist's natural desire to
round out his story perfectly. Truth may be stranger than fiction, but
it usually lacks what is known in literature as "construction." '[20]

In most ways, despite the Author's Note ending a highly constructed
novel, Barnes resists the desire to round out his story, instead pro-
secuting his motif of 'seeing' from George's myopia to his final
search for an absent Doyle through binoculars, from Arthur's desire
to see his grandmother's corpse to his desire to see a spirit world.
The lawyer and the novelist are separated by belief, however, and
the book suggests strongly that 'believing is seeing' from the police
case against George to Arthur's conviction that George is a victim of
'race prejudice'. On the evidence of the handwriting expert Thomas
Gurrin, George is found guilty of writing the letters, some of which
were supposedly posted under the door while he was inside the
vicarage, and this is just one example of the unresolved rather than
unsolved elements of the case, including the horsehairs on George's
clothing, the presence or absence of bloodstains, George's supposed
escape from his father's locked room, and so on.

Adapted for the stage by the playwright David Edgar in 2010,
Arthur & George is undoubtedly one of the most satisfying novels of
Barnes's career. It is a welcome addition to a substantial body of work
and reasserts Barnes's considerable powers as a novelist who is a skilled
fabulist and perennial experimenter, crafting complex and often
comical stories with understanding and irony. Formal and linguistic
play characterise the fiction but are combined with a fierce intelligence that resists both sentiment and simple answers, opposing the
oppressive authority of official accounts and the easy falsifications of
willed belief.

Notes

1 D. Michael Risinger, 'Boxes in boxes: Julian Barnes, Conan Doyle, Sherlock Holmes and the Edalji Case' in *International Commentary on Evidence* 4:2 (2006), pp. 1–90; Gordon Weaver, *Conan Doyle and the Parson's Son: The George Edalji Case*, Cambridge: Vanguard, 2006.

2 Dominc Head, 'Julian Barnes and the case of English identity' in Philip Tew and Rod Mengham (eds), *British Fiction Today*, London: Continuum, 2006, p. 16. There are of course times when Barnes's licence with history is interesting in terms of critical analysis. Risinger points out that Edalji's mother was not Scottish, as Barnes has her, but English. Head also refers to Charlotte Edalji as Scottish (p. 21) when discussing Barnes's analysis of the construction of Englishness, but the fact that she was English in real life may add a further twist to the novel's concern with those (especially Arthur and George) whose 'Englishness' is contested by themselves or others.

3 Zola's open letter to the French President Faure was published in the Paris newspaper *L'Aurore*.

4 Peter Costello, *The Real World of Sherlock Holmes: The True Crimes Investigated by Arthur Conan Doyle*, London: Robinson Publishing, 1991, p. 83.

5 Harry How, 'A day with Dr Conan Doyle' *The Strand Magazine: An Illustrated Monthly* IV (August 1892), pp. 182–8; reprinted in Harold Orel (ed.), *Sir Arthur Conan Doyle: Interviews and Recollections*, London: Macmillan, 1991, pp. 62–8.

6 Ibid., p. 66.

7 The report was published in the *Daily Telegraph* over two days on 11 and 12 January.

8 Shortly afterwards, George makes this same ironic misattribution (AG, p. 126), indirectly referring to the family as 'robust Hindoos'.

9 See especially the long discussion of spiritualism between Arthur and Jean in part three (AG, pp. 259–61).

10 A lack of imagination is also attributed to other characters in Barnes's fiction (e.g. Barbro Lindwall in 'The story of Mats Israelson', LT, p. 31).

11 Arthur Conan Doyle himself became well known for accepting as genuine several photographs of fairies. He also wrote a book on the subject in 1922 entitled *The Coming of the Fairies*.

12 This discourse is further underlined by the references to the case of Sophie Frances Hickman (AG, pp. 111, 116, 120, 129, and 313), a female doctor whose suicide was read at the time in terms of madness and degeneracy: see Susan Collinson, 'Sketches from the history of psychiatry: the case of the disappearing doctor', *Psychiatric Bulletin* 14 (1990), pp. 83–8.

13 Quoted in Daniel Stashower, *Teller of Tales: The Life of Arthur Conan Doyle*, New York, Owl Books, 1999, p. 251.

14 Quoted by Guignery, *The Fiction of Julian Barnes*, p. 59.

15 Cf. Arthur Conan Doyle, *Memories and Adventures*, Oxford: Oxford University Press, 1989, p. 215.

16 Gordon Weaver notes how 50 years later Maud Edalji 'drew attention to the colour prejudice of Captain Anson, whom she accused of objecting to anyone who had a skin darker than his own' (*Conan Doyle and the Parson's Son*, p. 344).

17 Doyle repeats the phrase to describe himself to Anson (AG, p. 269). He says his blood 'is mixed Scottish and Irish' (AG, p. 275).

18 Barnes says: 'I am constantly going into churches . . . to get a sense of what Englishness once was' (NF, p. 13).

19 This can be explored in numerous books, including Costello's *The Real World of Sherlock Holmes*, which considers one theory that George's brother Horace was the link between the family and its persecutors.

20 Stashower, *Teller of Tales*, pp. 258–9.

Select bibliography

Compiled by Claire Smith

Primary works
Publications details are given for editions quoted in this book. Date of first publication is given if a later editions is used.

Barnes, Julian, *Metroland* (1980; London: Robin Clark, 1981)
Barnes, Julian, *Before She Met Me* (1982; London: Picador, 1986)
Barnes, Julian, *Flaubert's Parrot* (1984; London: Picador, 1985)
Barnes, Julian, *Staring at the Sun* (1986; New York: Harper & Row, 1988)
Barnes, Julian, *A History of the World in 10½ Chapters* (London: Jonathan Cape, 1989)
Barnes, Julian, *Cross Channel* (1995; London: Picador, 1996)
Barnes, Julian, *Talking It Over* (1991; London: Picador, 1992)
Barnes, Julian, *The Porcupine* (1992; London: Picador, 1993)
Barnes, Julian, *Letters from London: 1990–5* (London: Picador, 1995)
Barnes, Julian, *England, England* (London: Jonathan Cape, 1998)
Barnes, Julian, *Love, etc* (London: Jonathan Cape, 2000)
Barnes, Julian, *Something to Declare* (London: Picador, 2002)
Barnes, Julian, 'Introduction' to Alphonse Daudet, *In the Land of Pain*. Translated and annotated by Julian Barnes. (London: Jonathan Cape, 2002)
Barnes, Julian, *The Lemon Table* (2004; London: Picador, 2005)
Barnes, Julian, *The Pedant in the Kitchen* (2003; London: Atlantic, 2004)
Barnes, Julian, *Arthur & George* (London: Jonathan Cape, 2005)
Barnes, Julian, *Nothing to Be Frightened of* (London: Jonathan Cape, 2008)

Secondary works

Books
Groes, Sebastian and Peter Childs (eds), *Julian Barnes: Contemporary Critical Perspectives*, London: Continuum, 2011.
Guignery, Vanessa, *The Fiction of Julian Barnes*, London: Palgrave, 2006.

Guignery, Vanessa and Ryan Roberts (eds), *Conversations with Julian Barnes*, Jackson: University Press of Mississippi, 2009.

Holmes, Frederick M., *Julian Barnes*, London: Palgrave, 2009.

Moseley, Merritt, *Understanding Julian Barnes*, Columbia: South Carolina: University of South Carolina Press, 1997.

Pateman, Matthew, *Julian Barnes*, Plymouth: Northcote House, 2002.

Sesto, Bruce, *Language, History, and Metanarrative in the Fiction of Julian Barnes*, Studies in Twentieth-Century British Literature, Vol. 3, Amsterdam: Peter Lang, 2001.

Shorter criticism

Amis, Martin, 'Snooker with Julian Barnes' in *Visiting Mrs. Nabokov and Other Excursions* (New York: Harmony Books, 1993), pp. 154–8.

Bentley, N., 'Re-writing Englishness: imagining the nation in Julian Barnes's *England, England* and Zadie Smith's *White Teeth*' in *Textual Practice* 21:3 (September 2007), pp. 483–506.

Bernard, Catherine, 'A certain hermeneutic slant: sublime allegories in contemporary English fiction', *Contemporary Literature* 38:1 (Spring 1997), pp. 164–82.

Brooks, N., 'Interred textuality: the "Good Soldier" and "Flaubert's Parrot (Ford Madox Ford, Julian Barnes)"' in *Critique – Studies in Contemporary Fiction* 41:1 (1999), pp. 45–51.

Buxton, Jackie, 'Julian Barnes's theses on history (in 10½ chapters)' in *Contemporary Literature* 41:1 (Spring 2000), pp. 56–87.

Candel Bormann, Daniel, 'Julian Barnes's history of science in 10½ chapters' in *English Studies* 82:3 (June 2001), pp. 253–61.

Cox, Emma, ' "Abstain, and hide your life": the hidden narrator of Flaubert's Parrot' in *Critique* 46:1 (Fall 2004), pp. 53–62.

Finney, B., 'A worm's eye view of history: Julian Barnes's A "History of the World in 10½ chapters"' in *Papers on Language and Literature* 39:1 (Winter 2003), pp. 49–70.

Goode, M., 'Knowing seizures: Julian Barnes, Jean-Paul Sartre, and the erotics of the postmodern condition' in *Textual Practice* 19:1 (September 2005), pp. 149–73.

Guignery, Vanessa, ' "Re-vision" and revision of sacred history in the first chapter of Julian Barnes's *A History of the World*' in *Alizes* 20 (July 2001), pp. 67–86.

Guignery, Vanessa, 'The narratee, or the reader through the looking glass in Julian Barnes's *Flaubert's Parrot*' in *QWERTY* 11 (October 2001), pp. 167–76.

Guignery, Vanessa, ed., *Worlds within Words: Twenty-first Century Visions on the Work of Julian Barnes*, a special issue of *American, British and Canadian Studies* 13 (December 2009).

Hamilton, Craig, 'Bakhtinian narration in Julian Barnes's *Talking It Over* and *Love, etc.*' in *Imaginaires* (University of Reims), 10 (2004), pp. 177–92.

Higdon, David Leon, '"Unconfessed confessions": the narrators of Graham Swift and Julian Barnes' in James Acheson (ed.), *The British and Irish Novel Since 1960* (London: Macmillan, 1991), pp. 174–91.

Miracky, James J., 'Replicating a dinosaur: authenticity run amok in the "theme parking" of Michael Crichton's *Jurassic Park* and Julian Barnes's *England, England*' in *Critique* 45:2 (Winter 2004), pp. 163–71.

Pateman, Matthew, 'Julian Barnes and the popularity of ethics' in Steven Earnshaw (ed.), *Postmodern Surroundings* (Amsterdam: Rodopi, 1994), pp. 179–91.

Pateman, Matthew, 'Philosophy in the courtroom: Barnes, Lyotard and the search for justice' in B. Axford and G. Browning (eds), *Postmodernity: From the Local to the Global* (Oxford: Oxford Brookes University Press, 1996), pp. 80–99.

Poree, Marc, 'Hidden facts since the foundation of the Ark' in *Critique* 522 (November 1990), pp. 900–10.

Rubinson, Gregory J., 'History's genres: Julian Barnes's *A History of the World in 10^1/$_2$ chapters*' in *Modern Language Studies* 30:2 (2000), pp. 159–79.

Salyer, Gregory, 'One good story leads to another: Julian Barnes's *A History of the World in 10^1/$_2$ chapters*' in *Journal of Literature & Theology* 5 (June 1991), pp. 220–33.

Scott, James B., 'Parrot as paradigms: infinite deferral of meaning in *Flaubert's Parrot*' in *Ariel: A Review of International English Literature* 21:3 (1990), pp. 58–68.

Semino, Elena, 'Representing characters' speech and thought in narrative fiction: a study of *England, England* by Julian Barnes' in *Style* 38:4 (Winter 2004), pp. 428–51.

Shepherd, Tania, 'Towards a description of atypical narratives: a study of the underlying organisation of *Flaubert's Parrot*' in *Language and Discourse* 5 (1997), pp. 71–95.

Stout, Mira, 'Chameleon novelist' in *New York Times Review of Books*, 22 November 1992.

Website

http://www.julianbarnes.com – Ryan Roberts's excellent website.

Index

A Dance to the Music of Time 50
A Passage to India 64
A Portrait of the Artist as a Young Man 144
A Room with a View (film) 114
Amis, Kingsley 5, 35
Amis, Martin 58
Amsterdam 106
Anger Generation 23
Animal Farm 108
Apocalypse 40
Aristotle 13
Austen, Jane 114

Barnes, Albert Leonard 2
Barnes, Jonathan 2
Barnes, Julian: Works
    A History of the World in 10¹/₂ Chapters 9, 12, 14, 15, 24, 53, 68, 71–83, 85, 130
    Arthur & George 6, 9, 12, 14, 38, 89, 106, 109, 110, 111, 117, 118, 129, 137, 139–58
    Before She Met Me 8, 9, 13, 34–45, 50, 53, 106
    Cross Channel 6, 12, 13, 22, 108, 110, 126–138
    England, England 6, 9, 12, 13, 14, 89, 106, 107, 108–25, 133
    Flaubert's Parrot 2, 9, 10, 12, 13, 14, 19, 46–59, 72, 80, 139

Letters from London 12, 13, 15, 107, 112
Love etc 14, 34, 72, 84–97, 106, 109
Metroland 2, 3, 4, 12, 13, 19–33, 34, 38, 42, 50, 54, 79, 129, 136
Nothing to be Frightened Of 2, 4, 6, 9, 11, 13, 24, 53, 89, 109, 126, 129, 131, 136, 137
Something to Declare 12, 13, 131
Staring at the Sun 2, 4, 9, 12, 13–14, 20, 34, 60–70, 136
Talking it Over 6, 12, 14, 34, 71, 84–97, 106, 127, 136
The Lemon Table 12, 13, 126–38
The Pedant in the Kitchen 6, 13
The Porcupine 14, 15, 82, 98–107, 108, 112
Barnes, Kaye Scoltock 2
Barth, John 7
Barthes, Roland 52, 55
Baudelaire 2, 23, 29
Beatles, The 23
Beckett, Samuel 47
Benjamin, Walter 74
Berlin Wall 82
Betjeman, John 4, 30
Big Issue 4
Blair, Tony 12
Boethius, 93
Borges, Jorge Luis 57
Bradford, Richard 5
Brel, Jacques 13

Brideshead Revisited (film) 113
Butler, Joseph 27
Byatt, A. S. 118

Cadman, Robert 65
Camus, Albert 56
Ceaușescu, Nikolai 112
Chamberlain, Joseph 147
Chandler, Raymond 4
Chaucer, Geoffrey 44
Cheever, John 4
Clough, Arthur 5
Coffee with Aristotle 2
Colet, Louise 55
Crichton, Michael 117
Criminal Court of Appeal 152

Daily Express 155
Daily Telegraph 108, 140, 141
Daudet, Alphonse 3, 13
David Copperfield 12
David, Elizabeth 13
De la Rochefoucauld, François 26, 60, 67
death 2, 3, 4, 15, 20, 21, 28, 30, 35, 37, 41, 49, 50, 53, 54, 55, 57, 58, 60, 62, 64–6, 68–9, 79, 80, 95, 106, 112, 126, 128–9, 132, 134, 136, 137, 140, 141, 142, 144, 148, 150, 154–5
Delius, Frederick 129
Dickens, Charles 47
Don Quixote 47
Drake, Francis 110
Dreyfus, Alfred 140, 150
Du Maurier, Daphne 39
Duffy novels 3–4, 10, 13, 44, 58
Durrell, Lawrence 7

Edgar, David 156
Eliot, George 47
Elizabeth (film) 115
Eyre, Richard 115

fabulation 6–9, 11, 14, 49, 52, 76, 78, 80, 121, 139
Falklands War 116
Fantasia of the Unconscious 40

Feydeau, Ernest 51
Fitzgerald, Penelope 5
Flaubert, Gustave 1, 2, 4, 11, 27, 46–59, 135
Ford, Ford Madox 8, 56, 133
Forster, E. M. 40, 64, 114
Foucault, Michel 57
Fowles, John 55, 108, 118
Freiburg, Rudolf 11
Freud, Sigmund 42
Fukuyama, Francis 103

Gargantua and Pangruel 47
Géricault, Théodore 79
Gorbachev, Mikhail 101, 104
Gormenghast 38
Great Expectations 19, 31
Greene, Graham 39
Guignery, Vanessa 14
Gurrin, Thomas 156

Hammett, Dashiell 4
Hardy, Thomas 5, 114
Hawes, James 116
Head, Dominic 139
Heart of Darkness 12
Hegel, G. F. 74, 80
Henry V (film) 115
Herbert, Juliet 135
Hewison, Robert 116, 117, 119
Hickman, Sophie 155
Higson, Andrew 113, 114
Hoffmann, E. T. A. 134
Holmes, Frederick 5, 10, 11
Honecker, Erich 98
Housman, A. E. 5
How, Harry 142
Howards End (film) 114
Howards End 40
Hugo, Victor 60
Husák, Gustáv 99, 112
Huxley, Aldous 36

If on a Winter's Night a Traveller 47
In the Land of Pain 3, 13
Ivory, James 114

J'Accuse 140
Jack the Ripper 155
Jackson, Glenda 12
James, Clive 3, 12
James, Henry 114
Jane Eyre 19
Jane Grigson 2
Jarrell, Randall 47
Johnson, Samuel 29, 121
Joyce, James 144
Jules et Jim 19, 86

Kádár, János 112
Kavanagh, Dan 3, 44
Khomeini, Ayatollah 107
Kierkegaard, Søren 68
Kipling, Rudyard 41, 147
Knowles, Enoch 155
Kondevo, Dimitrina 98
Kundera, Milan 47

L'Education Sentimentale 27
L'Etranger 20
La Ronde 86
Larkin, Philip 4, 5, 20, 30
Lawrence, D. H. 40
Lawson, Mark 9
Le Grand Meaulnes 19
Lee, Alison 46
Lenin, V I 102, 103
'Little Gidding' 20
Lively, Penelope 115
Lodge, David 7–9
Look Back in Anger 11
love 4, 5, 10, 11, 13, 14, 15, 21, 26, 32,
    34–44, 53, 54, 61, 71–5, 80, 81,
    85, 86–7, 90, 91–7, 130–1,
    132–4, 148
Lutyens, Edward 126

MacLean, Paul D. 36, 39
Madame Bovary 52
Major, John 12
Mallarmé 29
Married Love 62
Marx, Karl 74, 80

Maurice (film) 114
Maxwell, Robert 112
McEwan, Ian 106, 115
McEwan, Neil 117
Memories and Adventures 150, 153
memory 6, 7, 10, 15, 36, 50, 53, 61, 77,
    78, 89, 90, 93, 95, 109–11, 121,
    122, 123, 126–9, 133, 134, 136,
    142, 150, 155
Merchant, Ismail 114
Michelin Guide to France 2
Middlemarch 8, 12
Montaigne 2
Moore, Brian 6
Moseley, Merritt 44
Murdoch, Iris 7

National Gallery 24, 38, 79
New Review 3
New Statesman 3
New Yorker 107
Nietzsche, Friedrich 40
Nineteen Eighty-Four 108
North and South 12

O'Brien, Flann 47
O'Connor, Frank 4
Observer, The 3
Olivier, Laurence 115
Orwell, George 108
Osborne, John 11, 23
Othello 35, 43
Our Ostriches 62
Oxford 2, 3
Oxford English Dictionary 2, 3

Pascal, Blaise 75
Pateman, Matthew 5, 10
Peake, Mervyn 38
Possession 118
Potter, Dennis 4
Powell, Anthony 50
Proust, Marcel 113

Reagan, Ronald 104
Rebecca 39

Reisz, Karel 113
religion 10, 24, 54, 58, 60, 68, 73,
    75–80, 132, 145, 153, 154
Renault, Mary 117
Rhodes, Cecil 147
Rimbaud, Arthur 2, 19, 23, 25, 30
Robin Hood 12, 117
Roman Invasion 110
Royal Albert Hall 154
Rubinson, Gregory 10

Samuel, Raphael 118
Scholes, Robert 7–9
Self-Help 62
Shakespeare, William 11, 57, 115
Shostakovich, Dmitri 89
Sibelius, Jean 129, 130, 133
Simenon, Georges 13
Singing Detective, The 4
Sir Nigel 147
Smiles, Samuel 62
Smith, Logan Pearsall 58
Spencer, Stanley 42
Stashower, Daniel 155
Stein, Gertrude 62
Sterne, Laurence 47
Stopes, Marie 62
Stout, Mira 5, 10
Strand 141, 142
Stravinsky, Igor 89, 134
Sturridge, Charles 113
Sunday Times, The 3
Swift, Jonathan 47

Thatcher, Margaret 12, 107, 116
The Book of Laughter and Forgetting 47
The End of the Affair 39
The Fall 56
The French Lieutenant's Woman 55,
    118

The French Lieutenant's Woman (film)
    113
The Good Soldier 8, 56
The Less Deceived 20
The Order of Things 57
The Ploughman's Lunch (film) 115
The Remains of the Day (film) 114
The Umpire 149
The White Company 147
Thomson, Rupert 116
Tiananmen Square 82
Titanic 80
To the Lighthouse 12
Treaty of Rome 110
Trois Contes 47, 48
Truffaut, François 13, 19
Turgenev, Ivan 131, 132

Unsworth, Barry 115
Updike, John 4

Van Dyck 29
Verlaine, Paul 19, 25
Victoria 75
Voltaire 2
Vonnegut, Kurt 7

Waugh, Evelyn 3, 5, 113–14
Weaver, Gordon 139
Westworld (film) 117
Wilson, Angus 5, 35
Women in Love 40
Woolf, Virginia 135
Wright, Patrick 119

Yalom, Irvin 60
Yeats, W. B. 29

Zhelev, Zhelyu 99
Zhivkov, Todor 99, 112
Zola, Emile 1, 140, 151